Sex and the City

Candace Bushnell

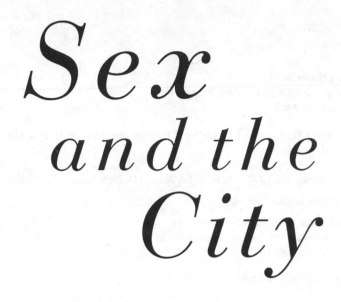

WARNER BOOKS

A Time Warner Company

Warner Books Edition
Copyright © 1996 by Candace Bushnell
All rights reserved.

This Warner Books edition is published by arrangement with Atlantic Monthly
Press, New York, NY

Warner Books, Inc.1271 Avenue of the Americas, New York, NY 10020

 A Time Warner Company

Printed in the United States of America
First Warner Books Printing: September 1997
First Reissue: July 1998

ISBN 0-7394-0981-6

Cover design by John Gall
Manhattan photo: UPI/Bettmann
Candace Bushnell photo: Uli Rose

For Peter Stevenson and Snippy, who once bit his teddy bear

And to all my friends

SEX
and the
CITY

1

My Unsentimental Education:
Love in Manhattan?
I Don't Think So . . .

Here's a Valentine's Day tale. Prepare yourself.

An English journalist came to New York. She was attractive and witty, and right away she hooked up with one of New York's typically eligible bachelors. Tim was forty-two, an investment banker who made about $5 million a year. For two weeks, they kissed, held hands—and then on a warm fall day he drove her to the house he was building in the Hamptons. They looked at the plans with the architect. "I wanted to tell the architect to fill in the railings on the second floor, so the children wouldn't fall through," said the journalist. "I expected Tim was going to ask me to marry him." On Sunday night, Tim dropped her off at her apartment and reminded her that they had dinner plans for Tuesday. On Tuesday, he called and said he'd have to take a rain check. When she hadn't heard from him after two weeks, she called and told him, "That's an awfully long rain check." He said he would call her later in the week.

He never did call, of course. But what interested me was that she couldn't understand what had happened. In England, she explained, meeting the architect would have meant something. Then I realized, Of course: She's from London. No one's told her about the End of Love in Manhattan. Then I thought: She'll learn.

Welcome to the Age of Un-Innocence. The glittering lights of Manhattan that served as backdrops for Edith Wharton's bodice-heaving trysts are still glowing—but the stage is empty. No one has breakfast at Tiffany's, and no one has affairs to remember—instead, we have breakfast at seven A.M. and affairs we try to forget as quickly as possible. How did we get into this mess?

Truman Capote understood our nineties dilemma—the dilemma of Love vs. the Deal—all too well. In *Breakfast at Tiffany's,* Holly Golightly and Paul Varjak were faced with restrictions—he was a kept man, she was a kept woman—but in the end they surmounted them and chose love over money. That doesn't happen much in Manhattan these days. We are all kept men and women—by our jobs, by our apartments, and then some of us by the pecking order at Mortimers and the Royalton, by Hamptons beachfront, by front-row Garden tickets—and we like it that way. Self-protection and closing the deal are paramount. Cupid has flown the co-op.

When was the last time you heard someone say, "I love you!" without tagging on the inevitable (if unspoken) "as a friend." When was the last time you saw two people gazing into each other's eyes without thinking, Yeah, right? When was the last time you heard someone announce, "I am truly, madly in love," without thinking, Just wait until Monday morning? And what turned out to be the hot non–Tim Allen Christmas movie? *Disclosure*—for which ten or fifteen million moviegoers went to see unwanted, unaffectionate sex between corporate erotomaniacs—hardly the stuff we like to think about when we think about love but very much the stuff of the modern Manhattan relationship.

There's still plenty of sex in Manhattan but the kind of sex that results in friendship and business deals, not romance. These days, everyone has friends and colleagues; no one really has lovers—even if they have slept together.

Back to the English journalist: After six months, some more "relationships," and a brief affair with a man who used to call her from out of town to tell her that he'd be calling her when he got back into town (and never did), she got smart. "Relationships in New York are about detachment," she said. "But how do you get attached when you decide you want to?"

Honey, you leave town.

LOVE AT THE BOWERY BAR, PART I

It's Friday night at the Bowery Bar. It's snowing outside and buzzing inside. There's the actress from Los Angeles, looking delightfully out of place in her vinyl gray jacket and miniskirt, with her gold-medallioned, too-tanned escort. There's the actor, singer, and party boy Donovan Leitch in a green down jacket and a fuzzy beige hat with earflaps. There's Francis Ford Coppola at a table with his wife. There's an empty chair at Francis Ford Coppola's table. It's not just empty: It's alluringly, temptingly, tauntingly, provocatively empty. It's so empty that it's more full than any other chair in the place. And then, just when the chair's emptiness threatens to cause a scene, Donovan Leitch sits down for a chat. Everyone in the room is immediately jealous. Pissed off. The energy of the room lurches violently. This is romance in New York.

THE HAPPILY MARRIED MAN

"Love means having to align yourself with another person, and what if that person turns out to be a liability?" said a friend, one of the few people I know who's been happily married for twelve years. "And the more you're able to look back, the more you're proven right in hindsight. Then you get further and further away from having a relationship, unless something big comes along to shake you out of it—like your parents dying.

"New Yorkers build up a total facade that you can't penetrate," he continued. "I feel so lucky that things worked out for me early on, because it's so easy not to have a relationship here—it almost becomes impossible to go back."

THE HAPPILY (SORT OF) MARRIED WOMAN

A girlfriend who was married called me up. "I don't know how anyone makes relationships work in this town. It's really hard. All the temptations. Going out. Drinks. Drugs. Other people. You want to have fun. And if you're a couple, what are you going to do? Sit in your little box of an apartment and stare at each other? When you're alone, it's easier," she said, a little wistfully. "You can do what you want. You don't have to go home."

THE BACHELOR OF COCO PAZZO

Years ago, when my friend Capote Duncan was one of the most eligible bachelors in New York, he dated every woman in town. Back then, we were still romantic enough to believe that some woman could get him. He has to fall in love someday, we thought. Everyone has to fall in love, and when he does, it will be with a woman who's beautiful and smart and successful. But then those beautiful and smart and successful women came and went. And he still hadn't fallen in love.

We were wrong. Today, Capote sits at dinner at Coco Pazzo, and he says he's ungettable. He doesn't want a relationship. Doesn't even want to try. Isn't interested in the romantic commitment. Doesn't want to hear about the neurosis in somebody else's head. And he tells women that he'll be their friend, and they can have sex with him, but that's all there is and that's all there's ever going to be.

And it's fine with him. It doesn't even make him sad anymore the way it used to.

LOVE AT THE BOWERY BAR, PART II

At my table at the Bowery Bar, there's Parker, thirty-two, a novelist who writes about relationships that inevitably go wrong; his boyfriend, Roger; Skipper Johnson, an entertainment lawyer.

Skipper is twenty-five and personifies the Gen X dogged disbelief in Love. "I just don't believe I'll meet the right person and get married," he said. "Relationships are too intense. If you believe in love, you're setting yourself up to be disappointed. You just can't trust anyone. People are so corrupted these days."

"But it's the one ray of hope," Parker protested. "You hope it will save you from cynicism."

Skipper was having none of it. "The world is more fucked up now than it was twenty-five years ago. I feel pissed off to be born in this generation when all these things are happening to me. Money, AIDS, and relationships, they're all connected. Most people my age don't believe they'll have a secure job. When you're afraid of the financial future, you don't want to make a commitment."

I understood his cynicism. Recently, I'd found myself saying I didn't want a relationship because, at the end, unless you happened to get married, you were left with nothing.

Skipper took a gulp of his drink. "I have no alternatives," he screamed. "I wouldn't be in shallow relationships, so I do nothing. I have no sex and no romance. Who needs it? Who needs all these potential problems like disease and pregnancy? I have no problems. No fear of disease, psychopaths, or stalkers. Why not just be with your friends and have real conversations and a good time?"

"You're crazy," Parker said. "It's not about money. Maybe we can't help each other financially, but maybe we can help each other through something else. Emotions don't cost anything. You have someone to go home to. You have someone in your life."

I had a theory that the only place you could find love and romance in New York was in the gay community—that gay men were still friends with extravagance and passion, while straight love had become closeted. I had this theory partly because of all I had read and heard recently about the multimillionaire who left his wife for a younger man—and boldly squired his young swain around Manhattan's trendiest restaurants, right in front of the gossip columnists. There, I thought, is a True Lover.

Parker was also proving my theory. For instance, when Parker and Roger first started seeing each other, Parker got sick. Roger went to his house to cook him dinner and take care of him. That would never happen with a straight guy. If a straight guy got sick and he'd just started dating a woman and she wanted to take care of him, he would freak out—he would think that she was trying to wheedle her way into his life. And the door would slam shut.

"Love is dangerous," Skipper said.

"If you know it's dangerous, that makes you treasure it, and you'll work harder to keep it," Parker said.

"But relationships are out of your control," Skipper said.

"You're nuts," Parker said.

Roger went to work on Skipper. "What about old-fashioned romantics?"

My friend Carrie jumped in. She knew the breed. "Every time a man tells me he's a romantic, I want to scream," she said. "All it means is that a man has a romanticized view of you, and as soon as you become real and stop playing into his fantasy, he gets turned off. That's what makes romantics dangerous. Stay away."

At that moment, one of those romantics dangerously arrived at the table.

A LADY'S GLOVE

"The condom killed romance, but it has made it a lot easier to get laid," said a friend. "There's something about using a condom that, for women, makes it like sex doesn't count. There's no skin-to-skin contact. So they go to bed with you more easily."

LOVE AT THE BOWERY BAR, PART III

Barkley, twenty-five, was an artist. Barkley and my friend Carrie had been "seeing" each other for eight days, which meant that they would go places and kiss and look into each other's eyes and it was sweet. With all the thirty-five year olds we knew up to their cuffs in polished cynicism, Carrie had thought she might try dating a younger man, one who had not been in New York long enough to become calcified.

Barkley told Carrie he was a romantic "because I feel it," and he also told Carrie he wanted to adapt Parker's novel into a screenplay. Carrie had offered to introduce them, and that's why Barkley was there at the Bowery Bar that night.

But when Barkley showed up, he and Carrie looked at each other and felt . . . nothing. Perhaps because he had sensed the inevitable, Barkley had brought along a "date," a strange young girl with glitter on her face.

Nevertheless, when Barkley sat down, he said, "I totally believe in love. I would be so depressed if I didn't believe in it. People are halves. Love makes everything have more meaning."

"Then someone takes it away from you and you're fucked," Skipper said.

"But you make your own space," said Barkley.

Skipper offered his goals: "To live in Montana, with a satellite dish, a fax machine, and a Range Rover—so you're safe," he said.

"Maybe what you want is wrong," said Parker. "Maybe what you want makes you uncomfortable."

"I want beauty. I have to be with a beautiful woman. I can't help it," Barkley said. "That's why a lot of the girls I end up going out with are stupid."

Skipper and Barkley took out their cellular phones. "Your phone's too big," said Barkley.

Later, Carrie and Barkley went to the Tunnel and looked at all the pretty young people and smoked cigarettes and scarfed drinks. Barkley took off with the girl with glitter on her face, and Carrie went around with Barkley's best friend, Jack. They danced, then they slid around in the snow like crazy people trying to find a cab. Carrie couldn't even look at her watch.

Barkley called her the next afternoon. "What's up, dude?" he said.

"I don't know. You called me."

"I told you I didn't want a girlfriend. You set yourself up. You knew what I was like."

"Oh yeah, right," Carrie wanted to say, "I knew that you were a shallow, two-bit womanizer, and that's why I wanted to go out with you."

But she didn't.

"I didn't sleep with her. I didn't even kiss her," Barkley said. "I don't care. I'll never see her again if you don't want me to."

"I really don't give a shit." And the scary thing was, she didn't.

Then they spent the next four hours discussing Barkley's paintings. "I could do this all day, every day," Barkley said. "This is so much better than sex."

THE GREAT UN-PRETENDER

"The only thing that's left is work," said Robert, forty-two, an editor. "You've got so much to do, who has time to be romantic?"

Robert told a story, about how he'd recently been involved with a woman he really liked, but after a month and a half, it was clear that it wasn't going to work out. "She put me through all these little tests. Like I was supposed to call her on Wednesday to go out on Friday. But on Wednesday, maybe I feel like I want to kill myself, and God only knows how I'm going to feel on Friday. She wanted to be with someone who was crazy about her. I understand that. But I can't pretend to feel something I don't.

"Of course, we're still really good friends," he added. "We see each other all the time. We just don't have sex."

NARCISSUS AT THE FOUR SEASONS

One Sunday night, I went to a charity benefit at the Four Seasons. The theme was Ode to Love. Each of the tables was named after a different famous couple—there were Tammy Faye and Jim Bakker, Narcissus and Himself, Catherine the Great and Her Horse, Michael Jackson and Friends. Al D'Amato sat at the Bill and Hillary table. Each table featured a centerpiece made up of related items—for instance, at the Tammy Faye Bakker table there were false eyelashes, blue eye shadow, and lipstick candles. Michael Jackson's table had a stuffed gorilla and Porcelana face cream.

Bob Pittman was there. "Love's not over—smoking is over," Bob said, grinning, while his wife, Sandy, stood next to him, and I stood behind the indoor foliage, trying to sneak a cigarette. Sandy said she was about to climb a mountain in New Guinea and would be gone for several weeks.

I went home alone, but right before I left, someone handed me the jawbone of a horse from the Catherine the Great table.

LOVE AT THE BOWERY BAR: EPILOGUE

Donovan Leitch got up from Francis Ford Coppola's table and came over. "Oh no," he said. "I totally believe that love conquers all. Sometimes you just have to give it some space." And that's exactly what's missing in Manhattan.

Oh, and by the way? Bob and Sandy are getting divorced.

2

Swingin' Sex?
I Don't Think So . . .

It all started the way it always does: innocently enough. I was sitting in my apartment, having a sensible lunch of crackers and sardines, when I got a call from an acquaintance. A friend of his had just gone to Le Trapeze, a couples-only sex club, and was amazed. Blown away. There were people naked—having sex—right in front of him. Unlike S&M clubs, where no actual sex occurs, this was the real, juicy tomato. The guy's girlfriend was kind of freaked out—although, when another naked woman brushed against her, she "sort of liked it." According to him.

In fact, the guy was so into the place that he didn't want me to write about it because he was afraid that, like most decent places in New York, it would be ruined by publicity.

I started imagining all sorts of things: Beautiful young hardbody couples. Shy touching. Girls with long, wavy blond hair wearing wreaths made of grape leaves. Boys with perfect white teeth wearing loincloths made of grape leaves. Me, wearing a super-short, over-one-shoulder, grape-leaf dress. We would walk in with our clothes on and walk out enlightened.

The club's answering machine brought me back to reality with a thump.

"At Le Trapeze, there are no strangers, only friends you haven't met yet," said a voice of indeterminate gender, which added that there was "a juice bar and a hot and cold buffet"—things I rarely associate with sex or nudity. In celebration of Thanksgiving, "Oriental Night" would be held on November 19. That sounded interesting, except it turned out that Oriental Night meant oriental food, not oriental people.

I should have dropped the whole idea right then. I shouldn't have listened to the scarily horny Sallie Tisdale, who in her yuppie-porn book, *Talk Dirty to Me,* enthuses about public, group sex: "This is a taboo in the truest sense of the word. . . . If sex clubs do what they aim to do, then a falling away will happen. Yes, as is feared, a crumbling of boundaries. . . . The center will not hold." I should have asked myself, What's fun about that?

But I had to see for myself. And so, on a recent Wednesday night, my calendar listed two events: 9:00 P.M., dinner for the fashion designer Karl Lagerfeld, Bowery Bar; 11:30 P.M., Le Trapeze sex club, East 27th Street.

MESSY WOMEN; KNEE SOCKS

Everyone, it seems, likes to talk about sex, and the Karl Lagerfeld dinner, packed with glam-models and expense-accounted fashion editors, was no exception. In fact, it got our end of the table worked up into a near frenzy. One stunning young woman, with dark curly hair and the sort of Seen-It-All attitude that only twenty year olds can pull off claimed she liked to spend her time going to topless bars, but only "seedy ones like Billy's Topless" because the girls were "real."

Then everyone agreed that small breasts were better than fake breasts, and a survey was taken: Who, among the men at the table, had actually been with a woman who had silicone implants? While no one admitted it, one man, an artist in his mid-thirties, didn't deny it strongly enough. "You've been there," accused another man, a cherub-faced and very successful hotelier, "and the worst thing is . . . you . . . liked . . . it."

"No, I didn't," the artist protested. "But I didn't mind it."

Luckily, the first course arrived, and everyone filled up their wineglasses.

Next round: Are messy women better in bed? The hotelier had a theory. "If you walk into a woman's apartment and nothing's out of place, you know she's not going to want to stay in bed all day and order in Chinese food and eat it in bed. She's going to make you get up and eat toast at the kitchen table."

I wasn't quite sure how to respond to this, because I'm literally the messiest person in the world. And I probably have some old containers of General Tso's Special Chicken lying under my bed at this moment. Unfortunately, all of it was eaten alone. So much for that theory.

Steaks were served. "The thing that really drives me crazy," said the artist, "is when I see a woman wearing one of those tartan skirts and high knee socks. I can't work all day."

"No," countered the hotelier, "the worst thing is when you sort of follow a woman down the street and she turns around and she is as beautiful as you thought she was going to be. It represents everything you'll never have in your life."

The artist leaned forward. "I once stopped working for five years because of a woman," he said.

Silence. No one could top that.

The chocolate mousse arrived, and so did my date for Le Trapeze. Since Le Trapeze admits couples only—meaning a man and a woman—I had asked my most recent ex-date, Sam, an investment banker, to accompany me. Sam was a good choice because, number one, he was the only man I could get to go with me; number two, he'd already had experience with this kind of thing: A million years ago he had gone to Plato's Retreat. A strange woman had come up to him and pulled out his unmentionable. His girlfriend, whose idea it had been to go there, ran screaming from the club.

The talk turned to the inevitable: What kind of people go to a sex club? I seemed to be the only one who didn't have a clue. Although no one had been to a sex club, everyone at dinner firmly asserted that the clubgoers would generally be "losers from New Jersey." Someone pointed out that going to a sex club is not the kind of thing you can just do, without a pretty good excuse, e.g. it's part of your job. This talk wasn't making me feel any better. I asked the waiter to bring me a shot of tequila.

Sam and I stood up to go. A writer who covers popular culture gave us a last piece of advice. "It's going to be pretty awful," he warned, though he had never been to such a place himself. "Unless you take control. You've got to take control of the place. You've got to make it happen."

NIGHT OF THE SEX ZOMBIES

Le Trapeze was located in a white stone building covered with graffiti. The entrance was discreet, with a rounded metal railing, a downmarket version of the entrance to the Royalton Hotel. A couple was coming out as we were going in, and when the woman saw us, she covered her face with the collar of her coat.

"Is it fun?" I asked.

She looked at me in horror and ran into a taxi.

Inside, a dark-haired young man, wearing a striped rugby shirt, was sitting in a small booth. He looked like he was about eighteen. He didn't look up.

"Do we pay you?"

"It's eighty-five dollars a couple."

"Do you take credit cards?"

"Cash only."

"Can I have a receipt?"

"No."

We had to sign cards saying that we'd abide by the rules of safe sex. We got temporary membership cards, which reminded us that no prostitution, no cameras, and no recording devices were allowed inside.

While I was expecting steamy sex, the first thing we saw were steaming tables—i.e., the aforementioned hot and cold buffet. Nobody was eating, and there was a sign above the buffet table that said, YOU MUST HAVE YOUR LOWER TORSO COVERED TO EAT. Then we saw the manager, Bob, a burly, bearded man in a plaid shirt and jeans who looked like he should have been managing a Pets 'R' Us store in Vermont. Bob told us the club had survived for fifteen years, because of its "discretion." "Also," he said, "here, no means no." He told us not to be worried about being voyeurs, that most people start off that way.

What did we see? Well, there was a big room with a huge air mattress, upon which a few blobby couples gamely went at it; there was a "sex chair" (unoccupied) that looked like a spider; there was a chubby woman in a robe, sitting next to a Jacuzzi, smoking; there were couples with glazed eyes (*Night of the Living Sex Zombies,* I thought); and there were many men who appeared to be having trouble keeping up their end of the bargain. But mostly, there were those damn steaming buffet tables (containing what—mini–hot dogs?), and unfortunately, that's pretty much all you need to know.

Le Trapeze was, as the French say, Le Rip-Off.

By one A.M., people were going home. A woman in a robe informed us she was from Nassau County and said we should come back Saturday night. "Saturday night," the woman said, "is a smorgasbord." I didn't ask if she was talking about the clientele—I was afraid she meant the buffet.

TALKING DIRTY AT MORTIMERS

A couple of days later I was at a ladies' lunch at Mortimers. Once again, the talk turned to sex and my experiences at the sex club.

"Didn't you love it?" asked Charlotte, the English journalist. "I'd love to go to a place like that. Didn't it turn you on, watching all those people having sex?"

"Nope," I said, stuffing my mouth with a corn fritter topped with salmon eggs.

"Why not?"

"You couldn't really see anything," I explained.

"And the men?"

"That was the worst part," I said. "Half of them looked like shrinks. I'll never be able to go to therapy again without imagining a bearded fat man lying naked and glassy-eyed on a mat on the floor, getting an hour-long blow job. And still not being able to come."

Yes, I told Charlotte, we did take our clothes off—but we wore towels. No, we didn't have sex. No, I didn't get turned on, even when a tall, attractive, dark-haired woman in her mid-thirties entered the rumpus room and caused a stir. She exposed her bottom like a monkey, and within minutes, she was lost in a tangle of arms and legs. It should have been sexy, but all I could think about were those *National Geographic* nature films of mating baboons.

The truth is, exhibitionism and voyeurism are not mainstream events. And neither, for that matter, is S&M, despite what you may have recently read elsewhere. The problem, in the clubs, anyway, always comes down to the people. They're the actresses who can never find work; the failed opera singers, painters, and writers; the lower-management men who will never get to the middle. People who, should they corner you in a bar, will keep you hostage with tales of their ex-spouses and their digestive troubles. They're the people who can't negotiate the system. They're on the fringes, sexually and in life. They're not necessarily the people with whom you want to share your intimate fantasies.

Well, the people at Le Trapeze weren't all pale, pudgy sex zombies: Before we left the club, Sam and I ran into the attention-grabbing tall woman and her date in the locker room. The man had a clean-cut, all-American face and was talkative: He was from Manhattan, he said, and had recently started his own business. He and the woman had been colleagues, he said. As the woman slipped into a yellow business suit, the man smiled and said, "She fulfilled her fantasy tonight." The woman glared at him and stalked out of the locker room.

A few days later, Sam called and I screamed at him. Then he asked, hadn't the whole thing been my idea?

Then he asked, hadn't I learned anything?

And I said yes, I had. I told him I had learned that when it comes to sex, there's no place like home.

But then you knew that, didn't you? Didn't you? Sam?

3

We Loved a Serial Dater

On a recent afternoon, seven women gathered in Manhattan, over wine, cheese, and cigarettes, to animatedly discuss the one thing they had in common: a man. Specifically, an Eligible Man of Manhattan, a man we'll call "Tom Peri."

Tom Peri is forty-three years old, five feet, ten inches tall, with straight brown hair. There is nothing remarkable about his appearance, save for a penchant, a few years ago, for dressing in black Armani suits paired with wacky suspenders. He comes from a wealthy manufacturing family and grew up on Fifth Avenue and in Bedford, New York. He lives in a modern high-rise on Fifth Avenue.

Over the last fifteen years, Peri, who is almost always referred to by his last name only, has become something of a legend in New York. He's not exactly a womanizer, because he's always trying to get married. Peri is, rather, one of the city's most accomplished serial daters, engaging in up to twelve "relationships" a year. But after two days or two months, the inevitable happens. Something goes wrong, and, he says, "I get dumped."

For a certain type of woman—thirtyish, ambitious, well placed socially—dating Peri, or avoiding his attentions, has become nothing less than a rite of passage, sort of like your first limo ride and your first robbery, combined.

Even among the city's other notorious ladies' men, Peri stands out. For one thing, he appears to be holding far fewer cards. He has neither the well-bred good looks of Count Erik Wachtmeister nor the free-flowing cash of Mort Zuckerman.

I wanted to know, What's Peri got?

Each of the women I contacted had been involved with Peri—either intimately or as an object of his ardent affections—and each said she had dumped him. None refused my request to get together for a session of Talking about Peri. Each woman, perhaps, had something . . . unresolved about Peri. Maybe they wanted him back. Maybe they wanted him dead.

"LIKE DARYL VAN HORNE"

We met at the home of Sarah, a filmmaker who used to be a model, "until I got sick of the bullshit and gained twenty pounds." She wore a dark pinstripe suit. "When you look over the list of guys you've dated, Peri is the one guy that doesn't make any sense," she said. "You think, What was that about?"

But before we could even get to the juicy bits, we made a disturbing discovery. Although none of the women had heard from Peri for months, that morning he had called four of them.

"I don't think he knows anything, I think it was just coincidence," said Magda. Magda has been friends with Peri for years—in fact, most of her girlfriends are former dates of Peri's, whom she met through him.

"He knows everything about us," one woman said. "He's like Daryl Van Horne in *The Witches of Eastwick*."

"Van Horney is more like it," said another. We opened the wine.

"The thing with Peri is this," said Sarah. "The reason he's so charming is, when you first meet him, he is articulate, he is funny—and, he's available at all times, because he doesn't work. What's more fun than a guy who says, 'Meet me for lunch,' then you go back to work, then he says 'Meet me for cocktails at six?' When was the last time you went out with a guy who actually wanted to see you three times a day?"

"'Cocktails' is such a loaded word," said Magda. "It's like Katharine Hepburn and Cary Grant."

Jackie, a magazine editor, said, "When I met him, we started seeing each other instantly—five nights a week. He won't leave you alone."

"He's smart, because the thing that he does is, he loves the phone," said Sarah. "Which to a woman, you think, He must really be into me, because he calls you ten times a day. And then you start to disregard the fact that he's like a funny-looking little thing."

"Then you start to look at his suspenders, and you think, My God," said Maeve, a poet who is half Irish.

"Then you begin to realize he's not funny," said Sarah. "He has a good stack of jokes, but once you've heard them a million times, they get really annoying. It's like a loop. He's looping himself."

"He told me that I was the only girl he ever went out with who got his jokes," said Maeve, "and I didn't think they were funny."

"And then you see his apartment. Those twenty-five door-men—what's that about?"

"You wonder why he doesn't just throw out all his furniture and go to the Door Store instead."

"Once he showed me these napkin holders he had gotten. They were in the shape of handcuffs. Like this was how he was going to seduce a girl, with napkin holders."

FIRST DATE: 44

So how does it all start?

Jackie's story was typical. "I was waiting for a table at Blue Ribbon," she said. "He walked up to me and started talking.

He was instantly funny. I thought, Omigod, we're really clicking. But I'll probably never hear from him again." Everyone nodded. After all, hadn't we all been there?

"He called at something like eight the next morning," Jackie said.

"'Want to go out to lunch?' he asked. He asks you to lunch at 44 the next day."

Sapphire, a blond divorced mom, laughed. "He didn't take me to 44 until the second day."

"While you think he's still funny and clever, he asks you to go away with him for the weekend," said Jackie.

"He asked me to marry him on something like the tenth day," said Sarah. "That was pretty quick, even for him."

"He took me to dinner at his parents' house on like the third date," said Britta, a tall, rangy brunette who works as a photo rep and is now happily married. "It was just me and his parents and the butler. The next day, I remember I was sitting on his bed, and he was showing me home movies of him as a kid. He was begging me to marry him. He was saying, 'See, I can be a serious guy.' And then he ordered some cheesy Chinese food. I thought, Marry you? What, are you smoking something?"

Ramona sighed. "On the other hand, I had just broken up with someone, and I was pretty upset. He was always there."

A pattern emerged. The women who had dated Peri had all just left their husbands or long-term boyfriends when Peri found them. Or, was it they who found him?

"He's rebound man," Sarah said, definitively. "It's like, 'Excuse me, are you broken? Let's get intimate.'"

"He's the emotional *Mayflower*," said Maeve. "He gets women from point A to point B. You arrive at Plymouth Rock feeling enormously better."

His ability to empathize was a strong point. The phrase "He's just like a girl" came up over and over again. "He reads more fashion magazines than most women," said Sapphire, "and he's much more willing to fight your battles than he is his own."

"He's extremely confident," Maeve continued. "I think it's a mistake when men present themselves as helpless idiots who can't even find their socks. Peri says, 'I'm totally secure. Lean on me.' And you think, What a relief! Really, it's all that women want. Most men don't understand that. At least Peri is clever enough to affect that."

And then there's the sex. "He's awesome in bed," said Sarah.

"He's unbelievably great at making out," said Sapphire.

"You thought he was awesome?" Jackie asked. "I thought he was awful. Can we please talk about his feet?"

Nevertheless, so far, Peri seemed to be the embodiment of the two things women always say they want most—a guy who can talk and be understanding like a woman, but who also knows how to be a man in the sack. So what went wrong?

PERI: SIZE (EIGHT) MATTERS

"It's like this," said Maeve. "As long as you're neurotic and crazy, he's great. But once he solves all your problems, he becomes the problem."

"He gets incredibly mean," said one woman. The others nodded.

"Once," said Jackie, "when I said I was a size eight, Peri said, 'There's no way you're a size eight. You're a size ten, at least. I know what a size eight looks like, and believe me, you're no size eight.'"

"He was always telling me to lose fifteen pounds," said Sarah, "and when I went out with him, that was the thinnest I'd been in years."

"I think when men tell women to lose weight, it's a diversion from their own lack of size in certain areas," one of the women added dryly.

Maeve remembered a ski trip to Sun Valley. "Peri did everything right. He bought the tickets, he booked the condo. It was going to be great." But they started fighting in the limo to the airport—they wanted to sit on the same side. By the time they got on the plane, the stewardess had to separate them. ("By that time, we were arguing about who got to breathe more air," Maeve said.) They fought on the slopes. On the second day, Maeve began packing her bags. "He said, 'Ha ha ha, there's a blizzard outside, you can't leave,'" Maeve recalled. "I said, 'Ha ha ha, I'm going to take a bus.'"

A month later, Maeve went back to her husband. Her situation was not unusual—many of the women ended up dumping Peri, only to go back to the men they had broken up with.

But that didn't mean that Peri went away. "There were faxes, letters, and hundreds of phone calls," said Sapphire. "It was sort of awful. He does have a huge heart, and he's going to be a great guy someday."

"I kept all his letters," Sarah said. "They were so touching. You could practically see the streaks of his tears on the pages." She left the room and returned seconds later holding a letter. She read aloud: "'You don't owe me your love, but I hope you'll have the courage to step forward and embrace mine. I don't send you flowers because I don't want to share or demean your love with objects not of my creation.'" Sarah smiled.

"WE'RE GETTING MARRIED"

Post-Peri, the women claimed they had uniformly done well. Jackie said she was dating her personal trainer; Magda had published her first novel; Ramona was married and pregnant; Maeve had opened a cafe; Sapphire had rediscovered an old love; Sarah said she was happy to be pursuing a twenty-seven-year-old boy-toy.

As for Peri, he recently moved abroad, in search of fresh marriage prospects. One of the women had heard he got dumped by an English woman who had really wanted to marry a duke. "He always dates the wrong women," Sapphire said.

Six months ago, Peri came back for a visit and took Sarah out to dinner. "He took my hand in his," she said, "and he was saying to his friend, 'She's the only woman I ever loved.' For old time's sake, I went back to his apartment for a drink, and he asked me to marry him so seriously, I couldn't believe it. I thought he was lying. So I decided to torture him.

"He told me, 'I don't want you to see any other men, and I won't see any other women.'

"I said, 'Okay,' thinking, How's that going to work? He lives in Europe and I live in New York. But the next morning, he called me up and said, 'You realize you're my girlfriend now.'

"I said, 'Okay, Peri, that's cool.'"

He went back to Europe, and, Sarah said, she forgot about the whole thing. One morning, she was in bed with her new boyfriend when the phone rang. It was Peri. While Sarah was talking to him, her boyfriend said, "Do you want some coffee?" Peri went nuts.

"Who's there?" he said.

"A friend," Sarah said.

"At ten in the morning? You're sleeping with another guy? We're getting married and you're sleeping with another guy?" He hung up, but a week later he called back.

"Are you ready?" he asked.

"For what?" Sarah said.

"We're getting married, aren't we? You're not still seeing someone, are you?"

"Listen, Peri, I don't see a ring on my finger," Sarah said. "Why don't you send a messenger over to Harry Winston's to pick something up, and then we'll talk."

Peri never called Harry Winston's, and he didn't call Sarah again for months. She said she sort of missed him. "I adore him," she said. "I feel compassion for him because he's totally fucked up."

It was getting dark outside, but nobody wanted to leave. They all wanted to stay, transfixed by the idea of a man like Tom Peri, but not Tom Peri.

4

Manhattan Wedlock:
Never-Married Women,
Toxic Bachelors

Lunch the other day. Vicious gossip with a man I'd just met. We were discussing mutual friends, a couple. He knew the husband, I knew the wife. I'd never met the husband, and I hadn't seen the wife in years (except to run into her occasionally on the street), but as usual, I knew everything about the situation.

"It's going to end badly," I said. "He was naive. A country mouse. He came in from Boston and he didn't know anything about her and she jumped at the opportunity. She'd already gone through so many guys in New York and she had a reputation. No guy in New York would have married her."

I attacked my fried chicken, warming up to the subject. "Women in New York know. They know when they have to get married, and that's when they do it. Maybe they've slept with too many guys, or they know nothing's ever going to really happen with their career, or maybe they really do want kids. Until then, they put it off for as long as they can. Then they have that moment, and if they don't take it. . . ." I shrugged. "That's it. Chances are, they'll never get married."

The other guy at the table, a corporate, doting-dad type who lives in Westchester, was looking at us in horror. "But what about love?" he asked.

I looked at him pityingly. "I don't think so."

When it comes to finding a marriage partner, New York has its own particularly cruel mating rituals, as complicated and sophisticated as those in an Edith Wharton novel. Everyone knows the rules—but no one wants to talk about them. The result is that New York has bred a particular type of single woman—smart, attractive, successful, and . . . never married. She is in her late thirties or early forties, and, if empirical knowledge is good for anything, she probably never will get married.

This is not about statistics. Or exceptions. We all know about the successful playwright who married the beautiful fashion designer a couple of years older than he is. But when you're beautiful and successful and rich and "know everyone," the normal rules don't apply.

What if, on the other hand, you're forty and pretty and you're a television producer or have your own PR company, but you still live in a studio and sleep on a foldout couch—the nineties equivalent of Mary Tyler Moore? Except, unlike Mary Tyler Moore, you've actually gone to bed with all those guys instead of demurely kicking them out at 12:02 A.M.? What happens to those women?

There are thousands, maybe tens of thousands of women like this in the city. We all know lots of them, and we all agree they're great. They travel, they pay taxes, they'll spend four hundred dollars on a pair of Manolo Blahnik strappy sandals.

"There is nothing wrong with these women," said Jerry, thirty-nine, a corporate lawyer who happened to marry one of these smart women, three years older than he is. "They're not crazy or neurotic. They're not *Fatal Attraction*." Jerry paused. "Why do I know so many great women who aren't married, and no great guys? Let's face it, the unmarried guys in New York suck."

THE M&MS

"Here's the deal," Jerry said. "There's a window of opportunity for women to get married in New York. Somewhere between the ages of twenty-six and thirty-five. Or maybe thirty-six." We agreed that if a woman's been married once, she can always get married again; there's something about knowing how to close the deal.

"But all of a sudden, when women get to be thirty-seven or thirty-eight, there's all this . . . stuff," he said. "Baggage. They've been around too long. Their history works against them. If I were single and I found out that a woman had gone out with Mort Zuckerman or 'Marvin' (a publisher)—the M&Ms—forget it. Who wants to be twentieth on that line? And then if they pull any of those other stunts, like children out of wedlock or rehab stays—that's a problem."

Jerry told a story: Last summer, he was at a small dinner in the Hamptons. The guests were in TV and movies. He and his wife were trying to fix up a forty-year-old former model with a guy who had just gotten divorced. The two were talking, and suddenly something came up about Mort Zuckerman, and then Marvin, and suddenly Jerry and his wife were watching the guy turn off.

"There's a list of toxic bachelors in New York," said Jerry, "and they're deadly."

Later in the day, I relay the story to Anna, who's thirty-six, and who has a habit of disagreeing with everything men say. All guys want to sleep with her, and she's constantly chewing them out for being shallow. She's dated the M&Ms and she knows Jerry. When I tell her the story, she screams. "Jerry is just jealous. He'd like to be like those guys, except he doesn't have the money or the power to pull it off. Scratch the surface and every guy in New York wants to be Mort Zuckerman."

George, thirty-seven, an investment banker, is another guy who sees the toxic bachelors as a problem. "These guys—the plastic surgeon, that *Times* editor, the crazy guy who owns those fertility clinics—they all take out the same pool of women and it never goes anywhere," he said. "Yeah, if I met a woman who had gone out with all those guys, I wouldn't like it."

KIDS—OR LINGERIE?

"If you're Diane Sawyer, you'll always be able to get married," said George. "But even women who are A's and A-'s can miss out. The problem is, in New York, people self-select down to smaller and smaller groups. You're dealing with a crowd of people who are enormously privileged, and their standards are incredibly high.

"And then there are all your friends. Look at *you*," George said. "There's nothing wrong with any of the guys you've gone out with, but we always give you shit about them."

That was true. All of my boyfriends have been wonderful in their own way, but my friends have found fault with every one of them, mercilessly chewing me out for putting up with any of their perceived, but in my mind excusable, flaws. Now, I was finally alone, and all my friends were happy.

Two days later, I ran into George at a party. "It's all about having children," he said. "If you want to get married, it's to have kids, and you don't want to do it with someone older than thirty-five, because then you have to have kids immediately, and then that's all it's about."

I decided to check with Peter, forty-two, a writer, with whom I've had two dates. He agreed with George. "It's all about age and biology," he said. "You just can't understand how immense the initial attraction is to a woman of child-bearing years. For a woman who's older, forty maybe, it's going to be harder because you're not going to feel that strong, initial attraction. You'll have to see them a lot before you want to sleep with them, and then it's about something else."

Sexy lingerie, perhaps?

"I think the issue of unmarried, older women is conceivably the biggest problem in New York City," Peter snapped, then thoughtfully added, "It provides torment for so many women, and a lot of them are in denial."

Peter told a story. He has a woman friend, forty-one. She'd always gone out with extremely sexy guys and just had a good time. Then she went out with a guy who was twenty and was mercilessly mocked. Then she went out with another sexy guy her age, and he left her, and suddenly she couldn't get any more dates. She had a complete physical breakdown and couldn't keep her job and had to move back to Iowa to live with her mother. This is beyond every woman's worst nightmare, and it's not a story that makes men feel bad.

ROGER'S VERSION

Roger was sitting in a restaurant on the Upper East Side, feeling good and drinking red wine. He's thirty-nine, and he runs his own fund and lives on Park Avenue in a classic-six apartment. He was thinking about what I'll call the mid-thirties power flip.

"When you're a young guy in your twenties and early thirties, women are controlling the relationships," Roger explained. "By the time you get to be an eligible man in your late thirties, you feel like you're being devoured by women." In other words, suddenly the guy has all the power. It can happen overnight.

Roger said he had gone to a cocktail party earlier in the evening, and, when he walked in, there were seven single women in their mid- to late thirties, all Upper East Side blond, wearing black cocktail dresses, and one wittier than the next. "You know that there's nothing you can say that's wrong," Roger said. "For women, it's desperation combined with reaching their sexual peak. It's a very volatile combination. You see that look in their eyes—possession at any cost mixed with a healthy respect for cash flow—and you feel like they're going to Lexis and Nexis you as soon as you leave the room. The worst thing is, most of these women are really interesting because they didn't just go and get married. But when a man sees that look in their eyes—how can you feel passionate?"

Back to Peter, who was working himself into a frenzy over Alec Baldwin. "The problem is expectations. Older women don't want to settle for what's still available. They can't find guys who are cool and vital, so they say screw it—I'd rather be alone. No, I don't feel sorry for anyone who has expectations they can't meet. I feel sorry for the loser guys who these women won't look at. What they really want is Alec Baldwin. There isn't one woman in New York who hasn't turned down ten wonderful, loving guys because they were too fat or they weren't powerful enough or they weren't rich enough or indifferent enough. But those really sexy guys the women are holding out for are interested in girls in their mid-twenties."

By now, Peter was practically screaming. "Why don't those women marry a fat guy? Why don't they marry a big, fat tub of lard?"

GOOD FRIENDS, LOUSY HUSBANDS

I asked that very question to Charlotte, the English journalist. "I'll tell you why," she said. "I've gone out with some of those guys—the ones who are short, fat, and ugly—and it doesn't make any difference. They're just as unappreciative and self-centered as the good-looking ones.

"By the time you get to your mid-thirties and you're not married, you think. Why should I settle?" Charlotte said. She said she'd just turned down a date with a beautifully eligible, recently divorced forty-one-year-old banker because his unmentionable was too small. "Index finger," she sighed.

Then Sarah beeped in. She'd just gotten money to make her first independent film, and she was ecstatic. "This idea of women not being able to get married? It's so small-minded, I can't even deal with it. If you want to get these guys, you have to shut up. You have to sit there and shut up and agree with everything they say."

Luckily, my friend Amalita called and explained it all to me. Explained why terrific women are often alone, and not happy about it, but not exactly desperate about it, either. "Oh honey," she cooed into the phone. She was in a good mood because she'd had sex the night before, with a twenty-four-year-old law student. "Everyone knows that men in New York make great friends and lousy husbands. In South America, where I come from, we have an expression: Better alone than badly accompanied."

5

Meet the Guys
Who Bed Models!

There was just the slightest stir as "Gregory Roque," the conspiracy filmmaker, slipped into the Bowery Bar on a recent Friday night. The auteur of such controversial films as *G.R.F.* (Gerald Rudolph Ford) and *The Monkees,* Mr. Roque was wearing a tatty tweed jacket and keeping his head down. Surrounding him was a swarm of six young women, new models with a well-known modeling agency. All of the girls were under twenty-one (two were as young as sixteen), and most of them had never seen Mr. Roque's films and, frankly, couldn't have cared less.

Functioning like two small tugboats in keeping the swarm moving and intact were the modelizers, Jack and Ben—two self-employed investors in their early thirties—men of nondescript features, save for the buckteeth of one and the stylish spiky haircut of the other.

At first glance, it looked like a merry group. The girls were smiling. Mr. Roque sat in a banquette, flanked by his beauties, while the two young men sat in the aisle chairs as if to ward off any unwelcome intruders who might try to talk to Mr. Roque or, even worse, steal one of the girls.

Mr. Roque would lean toward one or another girl, engaging in snippets of conversation. The young men were lively. But it wasn't quite as charming as it appeared. For one thing, if you looked closely at the girls, you could see the boredom pulling down their features like old age. They had nothing to say to Mr. Roque and even less to say to each other. But everyone at the table had a job to do, and they were doing it. So the group sat and sat, looking glamorous, and after a while, they got in Mr. Roque's limousine and went to the Tunnel, where Mr. Roque danced dispiritedly with one of the girls and then realized he was bored up to his eyeteeth and went home alone. The girls stayed for a while and took drugs, and then Jack, who had the spiky haircut, grabbed one of the girls and said, "You stupid slut," and she went home with him. He gave her more drugs and she gave him a blow job.

That sort of scenario is acted out just about every night in New York, in restaurants and clubs. There, one invariably finds the beautiful young models who flock to New York like birds, and their attendants, men like Jack and Ben, who practically make a profession of wining and dining them and, with varying degrees of success, seducing them. Meet the modelizers.

Modelizers are a particular breed. They're a step beyond womanizers, who will sleep with just about anything in a skirt. Modelizers are obsessed not with women but with models. They love them for their beauty and hate them for everything else. "Their stupidity, their flakiness, their lack of values, their baggage," says Jack. Modelizers inhabit a sort of parallel universe, with its own planets (Nobu, Bowery Bar, Tabac, Flowers, Tunnel, Expo, Metropolis) and satellites (the various apartments, many near Union Square, that the big modeling agencies rent for the models) and goddesses (Linda, Naomi, Christy, Elle, Bridget).

Welcome to their world. It's not pretty.

THE MODELIZERS

Not any man can become a modelizer. "To get models, you have to be rich, really good-looking, and/or in the arts," says Barkley. He's an up-and-coming artist, and he has a face like a Botticelli angel, framed by a blond pageboy haircut. He's sitting in his junior loft in SoHo, which is paid for by his parents, as are all the rest of his expenses, his father being a coat-hanger magnate in Minneapolis. That's good for Barkley, because being a modelizer isn't cheap—there are drinks at clubs, dinners, cab expenses from one club to another, and drugs—mostly marijuana, but occasionally heroin and cocaine. It also takes time—lots of time. Barkley's parents think he's painting, but he's too busy spending his days organizing his nights with models.

"Frankly, I'm kind of confused about this whole model thing," Barkley says. He's pacing around his loft in leather jeans, shirtless. His hair is just-washed and his chest has something like three hairs on it. Models love him. They think he's hot and nice. "You've got to treat them just like regular girls," he says. Then he lights up a cigarette and says, "You've got to be able to roll into a place and go right up to the hottest girl there—otherwise, you're finished. It's like being around dogs, you've got to show no fear."

The phone rings. Hannah. She's doing a shoot in Amsterdam. Barkley puts her on the speaker. She's lonely and she's stoned. "I miss you, baby," she moans. Her voice is like a serpent trying to crawl out of its skin. "If you were here right now I'd have your ding-dong down my throat. *Aaaaahhhh.* I love that so much, baby."

"See?" Barkley says. He talks to her, raking his fingers through his hair. He lights up a joint. "I'm smoking with you now, baby."

"There are two kinds of modelizers—those who are closing the deal, and those who aren't," says Coerte Felske, author of *Shallow Man,* a novel about a man who chases models.

Leading the pack are the supermodelizers—men who are seen with the likes of Elle Macpherson, Bridget Hall, Naomi Campbell. "There are guys like this any place models congregate—Paris, Milan, and Rome," says Mr. Felske. "These guys have status in the world of modeling. They can pick off models like clay pigeons. They burn 'em and churn 'em."

But not all modelizers are high profile. In Manhattan, a necessary stopping-off point for young new models, just being rich can be enough. Take George and his partner, Charlie. On any given night of the week, George and Charlie are taking a group of models, sometimes up to twelve, out to dinner.

George and Charlie could be Middle European or even Middle Eastern, but in truth they're from New Jersey. They're in the import-export business, and though neither is thirty yet, they're each worth a few million.

"Charlie never gets laid," says George, laughing, spinning around in his leather swivel chair behind a large mahogany desk in his office. There are oriental carpets on the floor and real art on the walls. George says he doesn't care about getting laid. "It's a sport," he says.

"For these guys, the girls are a trophy extension," confirms Mr. Felske. "Maybe they feel unattractive or are blindly ambitious."

Last year, George got a nineteen-year-old model pregnant. He knew her for five weeks. Now they've got a nine-month-old son. He never sees her anymore. Here's what she wants: $4,500 a month in child support, a $500,000 life insurance policy, a $50,000 college fund. "I think that's a little excessive, don't you?" George asks. When he smiles, the tops of his teeth are gray.

WILHELMINA GIRLS

So how does a guy get into George's position? "The girls travel in packs," explains Barkley. "It's a very closed group. The models hang out in posses and live in groups in model apartments. They don't feel safe unless they go out together. It's intimidating to a guy.

"On the flip side, it works to your advantage, because if there are twenty models in a place, the one you want is not going to be the most beautiful. You have more of a chance. If there's just one, she's the most beautiful, and she can work it. When you go up to one in a group of four or five, it makes that girl feel like she's better than the other girls."

The trick is meeting one girl. The best way is through a mutual friend. "Once a guy has access, once you get validated by one of the girls," says Mr. Felske, "then the guy gets beyond being an ordinary Joe."

Three years ago, George was at a club where he ran into a girl he knew from high school who was with a booker with an agency. He met some models. He had drugs. Eventually, they all went back to the models' apartment. He had enough to keep them going until seven in the morning. He fooled around with one of them. The next day, she agreed to see him again, but only if all the other girls could come, too. He took them all out to dinner. He kept going. "That was the beginning of the obsession," he says.

George knows all of the model apartments now—the places where, for five hundred dollars a month, a new model gets to sleep in a bunk bed in a cramped two- or three-bedroom apartment with five other girls. But he's got to keep up, because the girls come and go all the time, and you have to stay close to at least one girl in the apartment.

Still, there's a free-flowing supply. "It's easy," George says. He picks up the phone and dials a number.

"Hello, is Susan there?" he asks.

"Susan's in Paris."

"Oooooh," he says, sounding disappointed. "I'm an old friend of hers [in truth, he's known her for two months], and I just got back into town myself. Damn. Who's this?"

"Sabrina."

"Hey, Sabrina, I'm George." They chat for about ten minutes. "We're thinking about going to Bowery Bar tonight. Getting a group together. Do you want to come?"

"Ummmm. Sure, why not," Sabrina says. You can practically hear her thumb pop out of her mouth.

"And who else is there with you?" George asks. "Do you think they might want to come too?"

George hangs up the phone. "It's actually better if there are more guys than girls when you go out," he says. "If there are more girls, they get competitive with each other. They get quiet. If a girl is seeing a guy and she lets the other girls know, it can be a mistake. She thinks the girls she's living with are her friends, but they're not. They're girls she just met who happen to be in the same situation. Girls try to steal guys all the time."

"There are a lot of bambis out there," says Mr. Felske.

George says he has a system. "There's a hierarchy of sexual availability in the model apartments," he says. "Wilhelmina girls are the easiest. Willi tends to get girls who grew up in mobile homes or the East End of London. Elite—they have two apartments—one uptown, on 86th Street, and one downtown, on 16th. They keep the nice girls in the uptown apartment. The girls in the downtown apartment are 'friendlier.' Girls who live with Eileen Ford are untouchable. One reason is that Eileen's maid hangs up if you call.

"A lot of these girls live between 28th Street and Union Square. There's Zeckendorf Towers on 15th. And a place on 22nd and Park Avenue South. The older models who work a lot tend to live on the East Side."

A MODELIZER GLOSSARY

Thing = a model

Civilian = women who are not models

"We talk about it all the time, how hard it is to go back to civilians," says George. "You never meet them or make an attempt to meet them."

"It's easier to get a model into bed than it is to get a civilian with a career to put out," says Sandy. Sandy's an actor with brilliant green eyes. "Civilians, they want stuff from guys."

THINGS DISSECTED

Thursday night at Barolo. Mark Baker, the restaurateur and promoter, is throwing one of his special parties. Here's how it works: The promoters have a relationship with the agencies. The agencies know the promoters are "safe"—i.e., they're going to take care of their girls, entertain them. In turn, the promoters need the modelizers to take the girls out. The promoters don't always have the money to take the girls out to dinner. The modelizers do. Someone's got to feed them. The modelizer meets someone like Mr. Roque. Mr. Roque wants girls. The modelizers want girls and they also want to hang out with Mr. Roque. Everyone is happy.

Outside, on this Thursday night, there's pandemonium on the sidewalk. People pushing, trying to get the attention of a tall, mean-looking guy who could be part oriental, part Italian. Inside, the place is jammed. Everyone is dancing, everyone is tall and beautiful.

You talk to a girl with a fake European accent. Then a girl from Tennessee who just returned from a trip back home. "I was wearing bellbottoms and platform shoes, and my old boyfriend said, 'Carol Anne, what the hell are you wearing?' And I said, 'Get with it, honey. This is New York.'"

Jack slides by and starts talking.

"Even if they're dumb, models are very manipulative. You can split them into three types. One: The new girls in town. They're usually really young—sixteen, seventeen. They go out a lot. They might not work that much, they want something to do, they need to meet people, like photographers. Two: The girls who work a lot. They're a little older, twenty-one and up, they've been in the business for five years. They never go out, they travel a lot, you almost never see them.

And three: The supermodels. They're looking for a big-time guy who can do something for them. They're all obsessed with money, maybe because their careers are insecure. They won't even look at a guy who has less than twenty or thirty mil. Plus, they have the 'big girl' complex: They won't hang out with any girl who's not a top model, and they ignore other models or bitch about them."

You go down to the bathroom with Jack and hang out in the men's room. "By the time they get to be twenty-one, these girls have tons of baggage," says Jack. "They have a history: Children. Guys they've slept with. Guys you don't like. Most of them come from broken homes or fucked-up backgrounds. They're beautiful, but in the end, they don't do anything for you. They're young. They're uneducated. They have no values, you know? I prefer the older ones. You have to find one without baggage, and I'm on the search."

GET ONE, GET THEM ALL

"The trick is to get one big girl—like a Hunter Reno or a Janna Rhodes," says George. "These are girls who have done covers in Europe. If you get one, you can get them all. At a nightclub, you pay attention to the older girls. They always want to go home early because they have to get up and work. You walk them out to a cab, being a gentleman, then you go back in and attack the young ones."

"These girls just want to be comfortable," says Mr. Felske. "They're so young. They're just finding their way in a grownup world. They're not fully developed, and they meet these guys who know all the tricks. How hard can it be?"

Back in the loft, Barkley opens a bottle of Coke and sits on a stool in the middle of the room. "You think, Who's prettier than a model. But they're not so smart, they're flakey and fucked up, they're a lot looser than you think. It's way easier to screw a model than a regular girl. That's what they do all the time. It's the way regular people are when they're on vacation. They're away, so they do things they wouldn't normally do. But these girls are away all the time because they travel from place to place. So that's what they're like all the time."

Barkley takes a sip from his Coke and scratches his stomach. It's three in the afternoon, and he just woke up an hour ago. "These girls are nomads," he says. "They have a guy in every city. They call me when they're in New York, and I always imagine that they call someone else when they're in Paris or Rome or Milan. We pretend that we're going out when they're in town. We hold hands and see each other every day. A lot of girls want that. But then they're gone." Barkley yawns. "I don't know. There are so many beautiful girls around that after a while you start looking for someone who can make you laugh."

"It's amazing sometimes what you'll do to be with these girls," George says. "I went to church with one girl and her daughter. I've started to hang out with older girls almost exclusively. I've got to retire soon. They keep me from getting work done. They make me fuck up my life." George shrugged and glanced out the window of his 34th-floor office at the view of midtown Manhattan. "Look at me," he says. "I'm an old man at twenty-nine."

6

New York's Last Seduction: Loving Mr. Big

A fortyish movie producer I'll call Samantha Jones walked into Bowery Bar, and, as usual, we all looked up to see whom she was with. Samantha was always with at least four men, and the game was to pick out which one was her lover. Of course, it wasn't really much of a game, because the boy-friend was too easy to spot. Invariably, he was the youngest, and good-looking in that B-Hollywood actor kind of way— and he would sit there with a joyously stupid expression on his face (if he had just met Sam) or a bored, stupid look on his face, if he had been out with her a few times. If he had, it would be beginning to dawn on him that no one at the table was going to talk to him. Why should they, when he was going to be history in two weeks?

We all admired Sam. First of all, it's not that easy to get twenty-five-year-old guys when you're in your early forties. Second, Sam is a New York inspiration. Because if you're a successful single woman in this city, you have two choices: You can beat your head against the wall trying to find a re-lationship, or you can say "screw it" and just go out and have sex like a man. Thus: Sam.

This is a real question for women in New York these days. For the first time in Manhattan history, many women in their thirties to early forties have as much money and power as men—or at least enough to feel like they don't need a man, except for sex. While this paradox is the topic of many an analytic hour, recently my friend Carrie, a journalist in her mid-thirties, decided, as a group of us were having tea at the Mayfair Hotel, to try it out in the real world. To give up on love, as it were, and throttle up on power, in order to find contentment. And, as we'll see, it worked. Sort of.

TESTOSTERONE WOMEN, FOOLISH MEN

"I think I'm turning into a man," said Carrie. She lit up her twentieth cigarette of the day, and when the maître d'hôtel ran over and told her to put it out, she said, "Why, I wouldn't dream of offending anyone." Then she put the cigarette out on the carpet.

"You remember when I slept with that guy Drew?" she asked. We all nodded. We were all relieved when she had, because she hadn't had sex for months before that. "Well, afterwards, I didn't feel a thing. I was like, Gotta go to work, babe. Keep in touch. I completely forgot about him after that."

"Well, why the hell should you feel anything?" Magda asked. "Men don't. I don't feel anything after I have sex. Oh sure, I'd like to, but what's the point?"

We all sat back smugly, sipping tea, like we were members of some special club. We were hard and proud of it, and it hadn't been easy to get to this point—this place of complete independence where we had the luxury of treating men like sex objects. It had taken hard work, loneliness, and the realization that, since there might never be anyone there for you, you had to take care of yourself in every sense of the word.

"Well, I guess it's a lot of scar tissue," I said. "All those men who end up disappointing you. After a while, you don't even want to have feelings anymore. You just want to get on with your life."

"I think it's hormones," said Carrie. "The other day, I was in the salon getting a deep-conditioning treatment because they're always telling me my hair is going to break off. And I read in *Cosmo* about male testosterone in women—this study found that women who have high levels of testosterone are more aggressive, successful, have more sex partners, and are less likely to get married. There was something incredibly comforting about this information—it made you feel like you weren't a freak."

"The trick is getting the men to cooperate," said Charlotte.

"Men in this city fail on both counts," said Magda. "They don't want to have a relationship, but as soon as you only want them for sex, they don't like it. They can't just perform the way they're supposed to."

"Have you ever called a guy at midnight and said, 'I want to come over,' and had him say yes?" Carrie asked.

"The problem is that sex doesn't stay done," said Charlotte. She had a name for men who were fantastic lovers: Sex Gods. But even she was having trouble. Her most recent conquest was a poet who was terrific in bed, but who, she said, "kept wanting me to go to dinner with him and go through all the chat bit." He'd recently stopped calling: "He wanted to read me his poetry, and I wouldn't let him."

"There's a thin line between attraction and repulsion," she continued. "And usually the repulsion starts when they begin wanting you to treat them as people, instead of sex toys."

I asked if there was realistically any way to pull off this whole "women having sex like men" thing.

"You've got to be a real bitch," said Charlotte. "Either that, or you've got to be incredibly sweet and nice. We fall through the cracks. It confuses men."

"It's too late for sweet," Carrie said.

"Then I guess you're just going to have to become a bitch," Magda said. "But there's one thing you forgot."

"What?"

"Falling in love."

"I don't think so," Carrie said. She leaned back in her chair. She was wearing jeans and an old Yves Saint Laurent jacket. She sat like a man, legs apart. "I'm going to do it—I'm going to become a real bitch."

We looked at her and laughed.

"What's wrong?" she asked.

"You're already a bitch."

MEETING MR. BIG

As part of her research, Carrie went to see *The Last Seduction* at three in the afternoon. She had heard that the movie portrayed a woman who, in pursuit of money and hot sex and absolute control, uses and abuses every man she meets—and never has a regret or one of those expected "Oh my God, what have I done?" epiphanies.

Carrie never goes to movies—she had a WASPy mother who told her that only poor people with sick kids send their kids to the movie theater—so it was a big deal for her. She got to the theater late, and when the ticket taker told her the movie had already started, she said, "Fuck you. I'm here for research— you don't think I'd actually go see this movie, do you?"

When she came out, she kept thinking about the scene where Linda Fiorentino picks up the man in the bar and has sex with him in the parking lot, gripping a chain-link fence. Was that what it was all about?

Carrie bought two pairs of strappy sandals and got her hair cut off.

On a Sunday evening, Carrie went to a cocktail party thrown by the designer Joop—one of those parties that should be in a movie, with everyone crowded in and the gay boys so lively, and even though Carrie had to work the next day, she knew she'd eventually have too many drinks and go home too late. Carrie doesn't like to go home at night and she doesn't like to go to sleep.

Mr. Joop cleverly ran out of champagne halfway though the party, and people were banging on the kitchen door and begging the waiters for a glass of wine. A man walked by with a cigar in his mouth, and one of the men Carrie was talking to said, "Oooooh. Who is that again? He looks like a younger, better-looking Ron Perelman."

"I know who it is," Carrie said.

"Who?"

"Mr. Big."

"I knew that. I always get Mr. Big and Perelman mixed up."

"How much will you give me," Carrie asked. "How much will you give me if I go over and talk to him?" She does this new thing she's doing now with her short hair. She fluffs it up while the boys look at her and laugh. "You're crazy," they say.

Carrie had seen Mr. Big once before, but she didn't think he'd remember her. She was in this office where she works sometimes, and *Inside Edition* was interviewing her about something she wrote about Chihuahuas. Mr. Big came in and started talking to the cameraman about how Chihuahuas were all over Paris, and Carrie leaned over and tightened the lace on her boot.

At the party, Mr. Big was sitting on the radiator in the living room. "Hi," Carrie said. "Remember me?" She could tell by his eyes that he had no idea who she was, and she wondered if he was going to panic.

He twirled the cigar around the inside of his lips and took it out of his mouth. He looked away to flick his ash, then looked back at her. "Abso-fucking-lutely."

ANOTHER MR. BIG (AT ELAINE'S)

Carrie didn't run into Mr. Big again for several days. In the meantime, something was definitely happening. She bumped into a writer friend she hadn't seen for two months, and he said, "What's going on with you? You look completely different."

"I do?"

"You look like Heather Locklear. Did you get your teeth fixed?"

Then she was at Elaine's, and a big writer, a big one, someone she'd never met, gave her the finger and then sat down next to her and said, "You're not as tough as you think you are."

"Excuse me?"

"You walk around like you're so fucking great in bed."

She wanted to say, "I do?"—but instead she laughed and said, "Well, maybe I am."

He lit her cigarette. "If I wanted to have an affair with you, it would have to last a long time. I wouldn't want a one-night stand."

"Well, baby," she said, "you've got the wrong girl."

Then she went to a party after one of those Peggy Siegal movie openings and ran into a big movie producer, another big one, and he gave her a ride in his car to Bowery Bar. But Mr. Big was there.

Mr. Big slid into the banquette next to her. Their sides were touching.

Mr. Big said, "So. What have you been doing lately?"

"Besides going out every night?"

"Yeah—what do you do for work?"

"This is my work," she said. "I'm researching a story for a friend of mine about women who have sex like men. You know, they have sex and afterwards they feel nothing."

Mr. Big eyed her. "But you're not like that," he said.

"Aren't you?" she asked.

"Not a drop. Not even half a drop," he said.

Carrie looked at Mr. Big. "What's wrong with you?"

"Oh, I get it," said Mr. Big. "You've never been in love."

"Oh yeah?"

"Yeah."

"And you have?"

"Abso-fucking-lutely."

They went back to his apartment. Mr. Big opened a bottle of Crystal champagne. Carrie was laughing and carrying on and then she said, "I have to go."

"It's four A.M.," he said. He stood up. "I'm not going to let you go home now."

He gave her a T-shirt and boxer shorts. He went into the bathroom while she changed. She got into the bed and lay back against the down pillows. She closed her eyes. His bed was so comfortable. It was the most comfortable bed she'd ever been in in her life.

When he came back into the bedroom, she was sound asleep.

7

The International Crazy Girls

If you're lucky (or unlucky, depending on how you look at it), you might one day run into a certain type of woman in New York. Like a constantly migrating, brightly colored bird she's always on the go. And not in the mundane, Filofax-filled way. This woman travels from one international hotspot to another. And when she gets tired of the party season in London, when she's had enough of skiing in Aspen or Gstaad, when she's sick of all-night parties in South America, she might come back to roost—temporarily, mind you—in New York.

On a rainy afternoon in January, a woman we'll call Amalita Amalfi arrived at Kennedy International Airport from London. She was wearing the white fake-fur Gucci coat, black leather pants custom-made at New York Leather ("They're the last pair they made in this leather—I had to fight with Elle Macpherson over them," she said), and sunglasses. She had ten T. Anthony bags, and she looked like a movie star. The only thing missing was the limo, but she took care of that by prevailing upon a wealthy-looking businessman to help her with her bags. He couldn't resist—as virtually no men are able to resist Amalita—and before he knew what had hit him, he, Amalita, and the ten T. Anthony bags were crawling toward the city in his company-paid-for limousine, and he was offering to take her to dinner that night.

"I'd love to, darling," she said in that breathless, slightly accented voice that hints at Swiss finishing schools and palace balls, "But I'm terribly tired. I've really just come to New York for a rest, you see? We could have tea tomorrow though. At the Four Seasons? And then maybe a little shopping afterwards. There are a few things I have to pick up at Gucci."

The businessman agreed. He dropped her off in front of an apartment building on Beekman Place, took her number, and promised to call later.

Upstairs in the apartment, Amalita put in a phone call to Gucci. Affecting an upper-crust English accent, she said, "This is Lady Caroline Beavers. You have a coat on hold for me. I've just arrived in town, and I'll be picking it up tomorrow."

"Very good, Lady Beavers," the salesperson said. Amalita hung up the phone and laughed.

The next day, Carrie was on the phone with an old friend, Robert. "Amalita's back," she said. "I'm having lunch with her."

"Amalita!" Robert said. "Is she still alive? Still beautiful? She's dangerous. But if you're a guy and you sleep with her, it's like becoming a member of a special club. You know, she was with Jake, and Capote Duncan . . . all those rock stars, billionaires. It's a bonding thing. You know, the guy thinks, Me and Jake."

"Men," Carrie said, "are ridiculous."

Robert wasn't listening. "There aren't very many girls like Amalita," he said. "Gabriella was one of them. Marit too. And Sandra. Amalita's so beautiful, you know, and really funny, and very bold, I mean, she's incredible. You'll run into one of these girls in Paris, and they'll be wearing a see-through dress and it will drive you nuts and you see their pictures in *W* and places like that, and their allure keeps growing on you.

Their sexual power is like this amazing, dazzling force that can change your life, you think, if you can touch it, which you can't, which . . ."

Carrie hung up on him.

At two o'clock that afternoon, Carrie was sitting at the bar at Harry Cipriani, waiting for Amalita to arrive. As usual, she was half an hour late. At the bar, a businessman, his female associate, and their client were talking about sex. "I think men are turned off by women who have sex with them on the first night," the woman said. She was dressed in a prissy navy blue suit. "You've got to wait at least three dates if you want the man to take you seriously."

"That depends on the woman," said the client. He was late thirties, looked German but spoke with a Spanish accent—an Argentinian.

"I don't get it," said the woman.

The Argentinian looked at her. "You middle-class American women who always want to hook a man, you're the ones who must play by the rules. You can't afford to make a mistake. But there is a certain type of woman—very beautiful and from a certain class—who can do whatever she wants."

At just that moment, Amalita walked in. There was quite a stir at the door as the maître d' embraced her—"Look at you!" she said. "So slim. Are you still running five miles a day?"—and her coat and packages were whisked away. She was wearing a tweedy Jil Sander suit (the skirt alone cost over a thousand dollars) and a green cashmere shell. "Is it hot in here?" she said, fanning herself with her gloves. She removed her jacket. The entire restaurant gaped. "Sweetpea!" she said, spotting Carrie at the bar.

"Your table is ready," said the maître d'.

"I have so many things to tell you," Amalita said. "I have just barely escaped with my life!"

Sometime in April, Amalita had gone to London to attend a wedding, where she met Lord Skanky-Poo—not his real name—"but a real lord, darling," she said, "related to the royal family and with a castle and foxhounds. He said he fell in love with me instantly, the idiot, the moment he saw me in the church. 'Darling, I adore you,' he said, coming up to me at the reception, 'but I especially adore your hat.' That should have been a dead giveaway. But I wasn't thinking clearly at the time. I was staying with Catherine Johnson-Bates in London and she was driving me crazy, she kept complaining about my stuff all over her fucking flat . . . well, she's a virgo, so what can you expect? Anyway, all I could think about was finding another place to stay. And I knew Catherine had had a crush on Lord Skanks—she used to knit him scarves out of that horrendous worsted wool—and he wouldn t give her the time of day, so naturally, I couldn't resist. Plus, I needed a place to stay."

That night, after the wedding, Amalita basically moved into the Eton Square house. And, for the first two weeks, everything was great. "I was doing my geisha routine," Amalita said. "Back rubs, bringing him tea, reading the newspapers first so I could point out what was interesting." He took her shopping. They entertained, throwing a shooting party at the castle. Amalita helped him with the guest list, got all the right people, charmed the servants, and he was impressed. Then, when they got back to London, the trouble began.

"You know, I've got all of my lingerie that I've been collecting over the years?" Amalita asked. Carrie nodded. She knew all about Amalita's vast collection of designer clothing, which she'd been acquiring over the past fifteen years—knew it well, in fact, because she had had to help Amalita wrap it up in special tissues to be put in storage, a job that had taken three days. "Well, one evening he comes in when I'm dressing," she said. "'Darling,' he says, 'I've always wondered what it would be like to wear one of those merry widows. Mind if I . . . give it a try? Then I'll know what it feels like to be you.'

"Fine. But the next day he wants me to spank him. With a rolled-up newspaper. 'Darling, don't you think you'd get more out of life if you read this instead?' I asked. 'No! I want a good thrashing,' he said. So I complied. Another mistake. It got to the point where he would wake up in the morning, put on my clothes, and then he wouldn't leave the house. This went on for days. And then he insisted on wearing my Chanel jewelry."

"How did he look in it?" Carrie asked.

"Pas mal," Amalita said. "He was one of those beautiful English types, you know, you can never really tell if they're gay or straight. But the whole thing just got so pathetic. He was crawling around on his hands and knees, exposing his bum. And to think that before this I was considering marrying him.

"Anyway, I told him I was leaving. He wouldn't let me. He locked me in the bedroom, and I had to escape out the window. And I was stupidly wearing Manolo Blahnik spike heels instead of the more sensible Gucci ones because I let him fondle my shoes and the Manolos were the only ones he didn't like—he said they were last year. Then he wouldn't let me back in the house. He said he was holding my clothes ransom because of some stupid, itsy-bitsy phone bill I'd racked up. Two thousand pounds. I said, 'Darling, what am I supposed to do? I have to call my daughter and my mother.'

"But I had my trump card. I took his cellular phone. I called him from the street. 'Darling,' I said, 'I'm going to meet Catherine for tea. When I get back, I expect to see all my suitcases, neatly packed, on the front stoop. Then I'm going to go through them. If anything's missing—one tiny earring, one G-string, the rubber on the heel of any shoe—I'm going to call Nigel Dempster.'"

"Did he do it?" Carrie asked, somewhat in awe.

"Of course!" Amalita said. "The English are scared to death of the press. If you ever need to bring one to heel, just threaten to call the papers."

Just then, the Argentinian walked by the table. "Amalita," he said, extending his hand and giving her a little bow.

"Ah Chris. *Cómo está?*" she asked, and then they said a bunch of stuff in Spanish that Carrie couldn't understand, and then Chris said, "I'm in New York for a week. We should get together."

"Of course, darling," Amalita said, looking up at him. She had this way of crinkling her eyes when she smiled that basically meant bug off.

"Argh. Rich Argentinian," she said. "I stayed on his ranch once. We rode polo ponies all over the campos. His wife was pregnant, and he was so cute I fucked him and she found out. And she had the nerve to be upset. He was a lousy lay. She should have been happy to have someone take him off her hands."

"Miss Amalfi?" the waiter asked. "Phone call for you."

"Righty," she said triumphantly, returning to the table after a few minutes. Righty was the lead guitarist in a famous rock band. "He wants me to go on tour with him. Brazil. Singapore. I told him I'd have to think about it. These guys are so used to women falling at their feet, you have to be a bit reserved. It sets you apart."

Suddenly, there was again a flurry of activity at the door. Carrie looked up and quickly ducked her head, pretending to examine her fingernails. "Don't look now," she said, "but Ray's here."

"Ray? Oh, I know Ray," Amalita said. Her eyes narrowed.

Ray wasn't a man but a woman. A woman who could be classified, loosely anyway, as being in the same category as Amalita. She was also an international beauty, irresistible to men, but a nut case. A late-seventies model, she had moved to L.A., ostensibly to pursue an acting career. She hadn't landed any roles, but she had reeled in several well-known actors. And, like Amalita, she had a love child, rumored to be the offspring of a superstar.

Ray scanned the restaurant. She was famous for her eyes—among other things—which were huge, round, the irises of such a light blue they appeared almost white. They stopped on Amalita. She waved. Walked over.

"What are you doing here?" she asked, seemingly delighted, even though the two were rumored to be sworn enemies in L.A.

"I just got in," Amalita said. "From London."

"Did you go to that wedding?"

"Lady Beatrice?" Amalita asked. "Yes. Wonderful. All the titled Europeans."

"Durn," Ray said. She had a slight southern accent, which was probably put on, since she was from Iowa. "I shoulda gone. But then I got involved with Snake," she said, naming an actor well known for action films—he was in his late sixties but still making them—"and, you know, I couldn't get away."

"I see," Amalita said, giving her the crinkly-eye treatment.

Ray didn't seem to notice. "I'm supposed to meet this girlfriend a'mine, but I told Snake I'd meet him back at the hotel at three, he's here doin' publicity, and now it's nearly two-fifteen. You know, Snake freaks out if you're late, and I'm always *en retard*."

"It's just a question of handling men properly," Amalita said. "But I do remember that Snake hates to be kept waiting. You must tell him hello for me, darling. But if you forget, don't worry about it. I'll be seeing him in a month, anyway. He invited me to go skiing. Just as friends, of course."

"Of course," Ray said. There was an awkward pause. Ray looked directly at Carrie, who wanted to throw her napkin over her head. Please, she thought, please don't ask my name.

"Well, maybe I'll give her a call," Ray said.

"Why don't you do that?" Amalita asked. "The phone's right over there."

Ray departed, momentarily anyway. "She's fucked everybody," Carrie said. "Including Mr. Big."

"Oh please, sweetpea. I don't care about that," Amalita said. "If a woman wants to sleep with a man, makes the choice, it's her business. But she's not a good person. I heard that she wanted to be one of Madame Alex's girls, but even Alex thought she was too crazy."

"So how does she survive?"

Amalita raised her right eyebrow. She was silent for a moment—in the end, she was a lady through and through, having been raised on Fifth Avenue with a coming-out ball, the whole works. But Carrie really wanted to know. "She takes gifts. A Bulgari watch. A Harry Winston necklace. Clothing, cars, a bungalow on someone's property, someone who wants to help her. And cash. She has a child. There are lots of rich men out there who take pity. These actors with their millions. They'll write a check for fifty thousand dollars. Sometimes just to go away.

"Oh, please," she said, looking at Carrie. "Don't be so shocked. You always were such an innocent, sweetpea. But then, you've always had a career. Even if you were starving, you've had a career. Women like Ray and I, we don't want to work. I've always just wanted to live.

"But that doesn't mean it's easy." Amalita had quit smoking, but she picked up one of Carrie's cigarettes and waited for the waiter to light it. "How many times have I called you, crying, no money, wondering what I was going to do, where I was going to go next. Men promise things and don't deliver. If I could have been a call girl, it would have been so much easier. It's not the sex that's the problem—if I like a man, I'm going to do it anyway—but the fact that you'll never be on their level. You're an employee. But at least you might walk away with some cash."

She raised her eyebrows and shrugged. "My way, well, is there any future? And you've got to keep up. With the clothes and the body. The exercise classes. The massages, facials. Plastic surgery. It's expensive. Look at Ray. She's had her breasts done, lips, buttocks; she's not young, darling, over forty. What you see is all she's got."

She mashed her cigarette in the ashtray. "Why am I smoking? It's so bad for the skin. I wish you'd stop, sweetpea. But you remember? When I was pregnant with my daughter? I was sick. Flat broke. Sharing a bedroom with a student, for Christ's sake, in a lousy flat because that was all I could afford. $150 a month. I had to go on welfare so I could get medical care to have the baby. I had to take the bus to the county hospital. And when I really needed help, sweetpea, there were no men around. I was alone. Except for a few of my good girlfriends."

At that moment, Ray reappeared at the table, biting her lower lip. "D'y'all mind?" she said. "This girl's gonna show up momentarily, but in the meantime, I need a cocktail. Waiter, bring me a vodka martini. Straight up." She sat down. She didn't look at Carrie.

"Hey, I want to talk to you about Snake," Ray said to Amalita. "He told me he was with you."

"Did he?" Amalita asked. "Well, you know, Snake and I, we have an intellectual relationship."

"Do you now? And I just thought he was a pretty good fuck who was good with my kid," Ray said. "I ain't worried about that. I just don't think I can trust the guy."

"I thought he was engaged to somebody," Amalita said. "Some dark-haired woman who's having his baby."

"Oh shit. Carmelita or something like that. She's like an auto mechanic from nowhere'sville. Yew-tah. Snake was going skiing and his car broke down and he took it to a garage, and there she was with her wrench. And her needy slit. Naw. He's trying to get rid of her."

"It's very simple then," Amalita said. "You just get some spies. I have my masseuse and my maid. Send him your masseuse or chauffeur and then have them report back to you."

"Goddammit!" Ray screamed. She opened her large, red-lipsticked mouth and leaned back precariously in her chair, laughing hysterically. Her blond hair was nearly white, perfectly straight; she was a freak all right but amazingly sexy.

"I knew I liked you," she said. The chair thumped to the floor and Ray nearly crashed into the table. Everyone in the restaurant was looking. Amalita was laughing, almost hiccup-ping. "How come we're not better friends?" Ray asked. "That's what I want to know."

"Gee, Ray, I have no idea," Amalita said. She was just smiling now. "Maybe it has something to do with Brewster."

"That goddamned little shit actor," Ray said. "You mean, those lies that I told him about you because I wanted to get him for myself? Well, shit, honey, can you blame me? He had the biggest willy in L.A. When I saw the thing—we were out to dinner at a restaurant and he puts my hand on it under the table, and I got so excited I took it out of his pants and started rubbing it, and one of the waitresses saw it and started screaming 'cause it was so big and then we got thrown out—I said, that thing is mine. I ain't sharing it with anyone."

"He was pretty big," Amalita said.

"Pretty big? Honey, he was like a horse," Ray said. "You know, I'm an expert in bed, I'm the best any man ever had. But when you get to be my level, something happens. The average-sized cock just doesn't do anything for you any-more. Oh yeah, I'll sleep with those guys, but I tell 'em all, I've got to be able to go out and get my little bit of fun. My satisfaction."

Ray had only had three-quarters of her martini, but some-thing seemed to be happening to her. It was like the high beams were on, but no one was driving. "Oh yeah," she said. "I just love that filled-up feeling. Give it to me baby. Do me." She started rocking her pelvis against the chair. She half raised her right arm, closed her eyes. "Oh yeah, baby, oh yeah baby. Oh!" She ended with a squeal and opened her eyes. She was staring straight at Carrie as if she'd suddenly noticed her for the first time. "What's your name, honey?" she asked. And Carrie suddenly recalled a story about how Capote Duncan had had sex with Ray on a couch in the middle of a party in front of everyone.

"Carrie," she said.

"Carrie . . . ?" Ray asked. "Have I met you?"

"No," Amalita said. "She's a great girl. One of us. But an intellectual. A writer."

"You gotta write my story," Ray said. "I'm telling you, my life would be a best-seller. So much stuff has happened to me. I'm a survivor." She looked to Amalita for affirmation. "Look at us. We're both survivors. The other girls like us . . . Sandra . . ."

"She's in A.A. and works all the time and never goes out," Amalita said.

"Gabriella . . ."

"Call girl."

"Marit . . ."

"Went crazy. Detox, then Silver Hill."

"Tell me about it," Ray said. "I heard she freaked out on your couch and you had to take her to the bughouse."

"She's out now. Has a job. PR."

"Poor Relations, I call it," Ray said. "They want to use her for her social connections, but her eyes are so glazed over you can't hardly talk to her. She just sits there like a bug while they paw through her Rolodex."

Carrie couldn't help it. She laughed.

Ray glared at her. "Well, it ain't funny. You know?"

8

Manhattan Ménage! Seven Men Pop the Inevitable Question

I'm at dinner with a man. We're into a second bottle of 1982 Château Latour. Maybe it's our third date, maybe our tenth. It doesn't matter. Because, eventually, it always comes up. The Inevitable.

"Errrrrr," he begins.

"Yes?" I ask, leaning forward. He rests his hand on my thigh. Perhaps he's going to "pop the question." It's not likely, but then again, what is?

He begins again. "Have you ever . . ."

"Yes?"

"Have you ever . . . wanted to . . ."

"What?"

"Have you ever wanted to . . . have sex with another woman?" he asks, triumphant.

I'm still smiling. But there it is, sitting on the table like a puddle of vomit. I already know what's coming next.

"With me, of course," he says. "You know, a threesome." Then comes the kicker: "We could maybe get one of your friends."

"Why would I want to do that?" I ask. I don't even bother inquiring why he thinks one of my friends might be interested.

"Well, I would like it," he says. "And besides, you might like it, too."

I don't think so.

"A SEXUAL VARIANT"

New York is a place where people come to fulfill their fantasies. Money. Power. A spot on the David Letterman show. And while you're at it, why not two women? (And why not ask?) Maybe everyone should try it at least once.

"Of all the fantasies, it's the only one that exceeds expectations," said a photographer I know. "Mostly, life is a series of mild disappointments. But two women? No matter what happens, you can't lose."

That isn't exactly true, as I discovered later. But the threesome is one fantasy at which New Yorkers seem to excel. As one male friend of mine said, "It's a sexual variant as opposed to sexually deviant." Another option in a city of options. Or is there a darker side to threesomes: Are they a symptom of all that's wrong with New York, a product of that combination of desperation and desire particular to Manhattan?

Either way, everyone has a story. They've done it, know someone who did, or saw three people about to do it—like those two "top models" who recently pulled a male model into the men's room at Tunnel, forced him to consume all his drugs, and then took him home.

A ménage à trois involves that trickiest of all relationship numbers: three. No matter how sophisticated you think you are, can you really handle it? Who gets hurt? Are three really better than two?

Lured perhaps by the promise of free drinks, free joints, and free honey-roasted peanuts, seven men joined me on a recent Monday evening in the basement of a SoHo art gallery to talk about threesomes. There we found the photographer and 1980 ladies' man Peter Beard on his hands and knees. He was "collaging": painting shapes on some of his black-and-white animal photographs. Some of the photos had rust-colored footprints on them, and I remembered I had heard Peter was using his own blood. He was wearing jeans and a sweatshirt.

Peter is a sort of "wild man," about whom one hears stories. Like: He was married to 1970s superbabe Cheryl Tiegs (true); that once, in Africa, he was hogtied and nearly fed to some animals (probably not true). He said he would work while we talked. "I'm just doing work all the time," Peter said. "Just to ward off boredom."

Everyone made cocktails, and then we lit the first joint. Except for Peter, the men asked me to change their names for this article. "Using our real names wouldn't be good for our client base," said one.

We launched into the topic of discussion.

"It's an avalanche right now," Peter said. "I know some girls, one of whom I'm meeting tonight, who says that over 90 percent of her girlfriends have propositioned her. This is definitely a new phenomenon."

Peter dipped his brush in the red paint. The modeling industry, he said, seemed to be grooming women for threesomes. "Agents and bookers are pushing favors from the girls to get them bookings." Then he added, "All the models are getting stroked in the loo."

Tad, forty-one, a golden-boy architect, remained skeptical. "I think the numbers are being kept by the government census bureau." But he went on. "Women physically represent more sensuality and more beauty," he said. "So it's easier for a man to fantasize about two women together. Two men together is kind of a dry fantasy."

Peter looked up from his spot on the floor. "Women can sleep in the same bed, and no one thinks anything about it," he said.

"We applaud it," said Simon, forty-eight, the owner of a software company.

"It's very unlikely any of us would sleep in the same bed with each other. I just wouldn't do it," said Jonesie, forty-eight, an East Coast–based record executive. He looked around.

"The reason men don't do it is because most other men snore," said Peter. "Plus, it's not good for the nervous system."

"It brings up all kinds of deep-rooted fears," said Simon. There was a moment of silence while we looked around the room.

Peter broke the tension. "The underground reality of this is the biological rat studies," he said. "Density, stress, and the overcrowding of the niche structures. The first phenomenon of overcrowded rats is the separation of the sexes. And in this city, with all the lawyers and all the overcrowded niche structures, you have incredible pressure. Pressure fucks up the hormones; when the hormones are screwed up, there are more homosexuals; and homosexuality is nature's way of cutting down on population. All of these unnatural things we're talking about exponentially expand."

"That sums it all up," Tad said dryly.

"We're leading sensory-saturated lives," Peter said. "High density. Intensity. Millions of appointments. Millions of lawyer appointments. A simple thing is no longer fun. Now you have to have two or three girls, or exotic strippers at Pure Platinum."

"On the other hand, the reason to have multiple sex partners could just be curiosity," said Tad. "Without being overly analytical."

But Peter was on a roll. "How about insincerity?" he demanded. "There's less sincerity and less honesty. If you're really attracted to a girl, you don't want another girl. But nowadays, there is less sincerity."

"That might be," Jonesie said cautiously.

"When you meet people in New York, all you get is their bullshit," said Peter, not noticing that his paintbrushes were drying out. "You get all their stuff they tell you at parties. You get the same damn thing at these dinner parties until you just stop going."

"You cut down," Jonesie agreed.

"And you go into the bathroom, and you get a blow job from someone in the fashion industry," Peter said. There was a brief and, if I'm not mistaken, awed silence. Then more Peter: "It's not reality. It's not communicating. It's not sincere. It's just a moment in their stress-ridden lives."

"And I thought I just wanted to get laid," Tad said.

E-LOVE IN VAIN

That was exactly Tad's state of mind three years ago, when he experienced the most basic level of troilism—what he called an "E-love gropefest."

He had recently broken up with his girlfriend of five years. He found himself at a party and saw an attractive twenty year old. He followed her and watched her get into a cab. He got into his Mercedes. When the cab stopped at a light, he pulled up. They made a date to meet the following night at a club.

She showed up with a girlfriend named Andie. "Fortunately," said Tad, "Andie turned out to be out of her mind." She'd just gotten off a plane from Italy and was swanning around in a fox fur coat. After consuming E-tabs, the three went back to Tad's loft, drank champagne, smashed the glasses on the floor, groped. The twenty year old fell asleep, and Tad and Andie went at it, with the twenty year old next to them on the bed.

Peter jumped back in. "It's more experiences, every day, therefore you have to do more and constantly faster! And more!" he said. "It's going beyond carrying capacity, pushing our luck, inventing new niches, expanding . . ."

"It's like someone walking by with a tray of cookies and you take a couple off the tray," said Garrick, thirty, a guitarist with a downtown band.

Tad started to agree with Peter. "It's the whole idea of more," said Tad. "It's four breasts, not two."

Thankfully, Sam, an investment banker, arrived. Sam, forty-one, was the type of guy who was always saying he wanted to get married but often "forgot" to call back the women he was dating. So he was still single. Sam said he had had three-somes.

"Why did you do it?" we asked.

Sam shrugged. "It's variety. You get tired of being around anyone after a while."

Sam said there are three basic situations that lead to three-somes. One: The guy has been secretly lobbying for a long time to get his girlfriend into bed with another woman. The reason could be that he's bored, or he secretly wants to sleep with her friend.

Two: The girlfriend secretly wants to sleep with another woman, and gets her boyfriend to go along to make it easier for her to deal with it.

Three: Two women are into each other and plot to get the guy into bed.

Sam said he'd had a girlfriend, Libby, for about six months, and he talked himself into believing that she really wanted to have sex with her best friend, Amanda. Of course, the truth, which he now admits, is that he wanted to have sex with Amanda.

Under pressure, Libby finally agreed to engineer the evening. Amanda came over. They had wine. They sat on the couch. Sam told the two women to take their clothes off. And then? "I was a complete failure," said Sam. While Libby remained on the couch, drinking wine, Sam took Amanda to bed. "I was totally into her. The problem is, you usually end up preferring one woman over the other, and then the other one gets left out," he said. Finally, Libby came over to the bed. "I guess they wanted me to tell them what to do, to take control of the situation. But I was so into Amanda, I couldn't do it," Sam said. Libby never got over it. Two months later, Sam and Libby broke up. Libby and Amanda didn't talk for a while.

Sam admitted that he knew there could be "consequences" from the threesome, but "you go ahead, anyway, because you're a guy."

Rule number one of threesomes: "Never, ever do it with your girlfriend," said Garrick. "It's always a disaster."

Rule number two: "You can't plan it. Something always goes wrong," said Simon, who said he had been involved in six or seven threesomes. "It has to be spontaneous."

Before we got to rule number three, the buzzer rang. Jim, a twenty-one–year-old magician, and Ian, a twenty-five-year-old television producer, arrived. Jim announced that he had been involved in a threesome the week before. "You get to tell your friends afterwards," he said.

"It was kind of cheesy," he said, "because the three of us had just seen the movie *Threesome*."

But before he could continue, the buzzer rang again. We all looked at each other. "Who's that?" All of the men who were supposed to be there had already arrived.

Peter looked up from his painting. "It's another woman," he said calmly.

I went upstairs to open the door. It was another woman, all right. We stared at each other in mutual surprise. "What are you doing here?" she asked.

"I was about to ask you the same question," I said. Then we did what women in New York always do, no matter how they really feel: We kissed each other on the cheek.

"Hello, Chloe," I said.

She was wearing a leopard-print jacket and a pink scarf. She is a sort of well-known girl-around-town, one of those women who are gorgeous, but you never know how she will end.

The men watched us walk down the stairs. Jim leaned back in his chair. "Now we might see some action," he said.

Chloe and I looked at each other. "I don't think so," we said.

Chloe surveyed the room. "This looks like an intervention," she said. Someone fixed her a vodka. I told her what we were talking about.

"I think every girl's least favorite thing is a threesome," Chloe said. She said it like she was talking about hair accessories. "Girls like one-on-one," she said. "They like the attention."

She took a sip of vodka: "I've been put in that position so many fucking times where a man wants a threesome. I was just with this boyfriend. We were with this other couple. They all wanted to play some kind of S&M game. I was put in the bedroom with the other woman's husband, whom I'd known for years. We looked at each other, and I said, 'This is never going to work because we're both submissives. It's a joke. We cancel each other out.'"

I wanted to know what happened if the two women in a threesome ignored the man.

"I pray for it," said Simon.

"That's what we all want," said Tad. "It's the real thing. It's like having a live movie in your bed. You do the work to get the two women together."

Jonesie seemed to be convinced that it worked a little differently. He kept using the word "pro." We weren't sure if he meant an actual prostitute who specialized in threesomes or something else.

"Usually, these things happen because the pro really wants to sleep with the woman," Jonesie said. "She's actually a lesbian, but she'll sleep with a man to get the woman. The pro is going to deal with you as best she can, and keep you going for as long as she can, so the other woman, whom she really wants, doesn't get nervous that she's been aggressively sold out by the guy. The pro will keep you going as long as she can until she finishes you off. Then she devours the other woman."

"I reject that," Simon said. "Jonesie's had a narrow range of experience."

"IMAGINE SAYING NO"

"One of the girls in my threesome; she loved to have sex," Jim said. "She'd had sex with all the guys we know."

"Wait a minute," Chloe interrupted. "How do you know she actually had sex with them?"

"Because Ian had sex with her," Jim said. "Ian had sex with her, and he said she loved to have sex with every guy."

"But how does he know?" Chloe said, indignant. "Maybe she only liked having sex with him. That's what's wrong with you guys."

"Her idea is that she can be like a guy," explained Ian. "Her idea is: Why do women have to be different from men? If a man can have sex with every girl he wants, why can't she have sex with every guy she wants?"

"Look at Simon," Jonesie said. "He wants her name and phone number right now."

Jim continued: "The other girl was the opposite of the first girl. She was kind of virginal. She'd had two boyfriends in her whole life. Anyway, these two girls had moved in together. And the crazy girl changed the life of the virginal girl, because a week later, the virginal girl was ready to sleep with everyone.

"We're all good friends," Jim said. "I had slept with the crazy girl, and the virginal girl was a girl I'd been pursuing for a year. We went to see a movie, and afterwards we got a bottle of wine and went to their apartment. We drank the whole bottle of wine."

"But that's only three and a half glasses," Chloe objected.

"There was a time when you, too, Chloe, could get drunk off of three and a half glasses of wine," Tad said.

"Okay," Jim said. "So we went back to their apartment and drank the teeny, tiny, little bit of wine that we had, and afterward, me and the crazy girl went into the bedroom—it was one of those bedrooms where the bed takes up the whole space so the only place to hang out is on the bed. So me and the crazy girl started fooling around. She wanted the other girl. And I wanted the other girl. We were both looking at her. She was walking around the apartment, trying to do her own thing. Walking into the bathroom and then the kitchen. Back and forth."

"What did she have on?" Simon asked.

"I don't remember," Jim said. "But we finally grabbed her hand and pulled her into the bedroom."

"And then you raped her," Simon said.

Jim shook his head. "Nooooo. We sat her down on the bed and just started touching her. Rubbing her back. Then we pulled her down onto the bed. The two girls were apart, so I just started putting one girl's hand on the other one's chest. And then the girls got into it. I was still involved, but I was trying to creep away, just to watch. After that, they went around and did it with everyone in New York. They probably did it with twenty guys from Buddha Bar."

Ian also had a story. "One time, I was having sex with a girl and there was another girl in the bed," he said. "At one point, I looked at this other girl and our eyes locked. And for the next five minutes, we were just staring at each other. That was the kicker. That's when it was great. That was intimate."

Peter Beard, who had been uncharacteristically quiet, suddenly spoke up. "Imagine saying no to a threesome," he said. "What an asshole you'd have to be."

"IT'S SPORT"

"But you don't really want to do it with a girl you care about," said Tad.

"The best is when you do it with a girl who's a great friend and a player," said Ian.

"And that's the reason why men want to have a threesome with you," Tad said to Chloe. "You're a great friend."

Chloe glared.

And then, pretty much out of the blue, Ian made an announcement. "I've been in more situations when it's two guys and one girl." He quickly added: "And I haven't participated in having sex with the other guy."

There was a moment of stunned silence. I wasn't quite sure that I'd heard correctly.

"It's the easiest way to do it," Ian shrugged. "It's sport. You don't care for that girl; otherwise, you wouldn't let your buddy have sex with her. It's not like she means anything to you."

"And it's a lot cheaper," Sam, the investment banker, piped in.

I thought of a few female friends of mine who had confessed to me the occasional fantasy of being with two men. I decided to tell them it's best to leave it a fantasy.

Chloe was still skeptical. "I've never had two men try to do that," she said. "Besides, men are so fucking competitive with each other, you'd think they wouldn't be able to deal with it."

"I wouldn't want to have sex with a woman after another man had been with her," said Peter.

Tad disagreed. "If it's my best friend, anything goes."

"Totally," Ian said.

"I could care who goes first, or what happens," Tad said.

"It's a conspiracy between the two guys," said Ian. "It's a one-on-one thing with your buddy. You're wondering with your buddy if you're going to be able to pull it off. And when you pull it off you're like—yeah!"

Jim was shaking his head violently. "I disagree."

"Jim, how can you say you disagree?" Ian asked.

"Yeah," Tad said. "You did it once with Ian."

"It's the idea of it that I don't like," Jim said.

Ian pointed at Jim. "But he was pushing me up to the girl," Ian said.

"A BAD VIBE"

Garrick spoke up. He said he had had about ten threesomes— "Hey, I'm thirty-five, a lot of shit has happened to me"— and several were with another guy. "It was always with my best friend, Bill," he said.

Bill was a model, and Garrick and Bill met at a gym downtown when Bill asked Garrick to spot him on the bench press. "Most of the guys who worked out there were gay," said Garrick. "So after that, it was like we were going out of our way to prove we weren't gay. The three-way was almost a validation of our heterosexuality. You're validating your masculinity to another guy.

"With me and Bill, it was about the thrill of the freak show," Garrick said. "Sometimes both of us had intercourse with the girl at the same time. Once a woman's submitted to that role of being with two guys, she's pretty much open to anything."

Garrick leaned forward in his chair and took a drag of his cigarette. "Bill once did it with another guy," he said. He laughed. "I always kid him about it. There was interaction between them. I don't know. To me, that constitutes latent homosexual yearnings. Do I have those yearnings? I don't know. Maybe Bill wasn't my type."

The younger men got kind of quiet.

Instead, Peter spoke. "I'm not a homophobe—I did happen to be in a situation with my best friend once and another woman. They were sleeping in a queen-sized bed in the same room. And I remember the vibes of sex. And when it was over, his hand was burned. Even though he was my best friend, I saw that he was an extra man on the scene, and it was such a bad vibe. I just remember pushing his burned hand away. It was such a bad vibe."

We all sat back for a moment. It was getting late. Almost time to go for dinner.

"Aw, I don't know," Garrick said. "I'm convinced threesomes are good for your psyche emotionally. It's such an atypical sexual experience, it's almost like it doesn't count. As soon as it's over, you don't think about it. If you cheat on your wife or girlfriend, you usually feel guilt afterwards. With this, there's no way you're going to have an ongoing relationship, so it's no threat.

"Besides," Garrick continued, "it brings you closer to the guy. Cements the relationship. What else can you do that even comes close? You're sharing the most intimate experience."

And what about afterward? The next morning?

"Oh, no problem. I remember, once, we all went to breakfast," Garrick said. "I remember it, because I paid."

9

What Has Two Wheels, Wears Seersucker, and Makes a Sucker of Me? A Bicycle Boy

A few weeks back, I had an encounter with a Bicycle Boy. It happened at a book party that was held in a great marble hall on a tree-lined street. While I was surreptitiously stuffing my face with smoked salmon, a writer friend, a guy, rushed up and said, "I've just been talking to the most interesting man."

"Oh yeah? Where?" I asked, glancing around the room with suspicion.

"He used to be an archaeologist, and now he writes science books . . . fascinating."

"Say no more," I said. I had already spotted the man in question—he was dressed in what I imagined was the city version of a safari suit: khaki trousers, a cream-checked shirt, and a slightly shabby tweed jacket. His gray-blond hair was raked back from his forehead, exposing a handsome chipped profile. So I was motoring, as much as you can motor in strappy high-heeled sandals, across the room. He was in deep conversation with a middle-aged man, but I quickly took care of the situation. "You," I said. "Someone just told me you were fascinating. I hope you won't disappoint me." I bore him off to an open window, where I plied him with cigarettes and cheap red wine. After twenty minutes, I left him to go meet some friends for dinner.

The next morning, he called me while I was still in bed with a hangover. Let's call him Horace Eccles. He talked about romance. It was nice to lie in bed with my head throbbing and a handsome man cooing into my ear. We arranged to meet for dinner.

The trouble began almost immediately. First he called to say he was going to be an hour early. Then he called back to say he wasn't. Then he called to say he was going to be half an hour late. Then he called and said he was just around the corner. Then he really was forty-five minutes late.

And then he turned up on his bicycle.

I didn't realize this at first. All I noticed was a more than normal dishevelment (for a writer) and a slight breathiness, which I attributed to the fact that he was in my presence. "Where do you want to have dinner?" he asked.

"I've already arranged it," I said. "Elaine's."

His face twisted. "But I thought we'd just have dinner at some neighborhood place around the corner."

I gave him one of my looks and said, "I don't have dinner at neighborhood places around the corner." For a moment, it looked like it was going to be a standoff. Finally, he blurted out, "But I came on my bicycle, you see."

I turned around and stared at the offending piece of machinery, which was tethered to a lamppost.

"I don't think so," I said.

MR. NEW YORKER AND
HIS THREE-SPEED

This was not my first encounter with a Manhattan literary-romantic subspecies I've come to call the Bicycle Boys. A while back, I was at a dinner with one of the most famous Bicycle Boys, whom we'll just call Mr. New Yorker. Mr. New Yorker, an editor at that publication, looks like he's thirty-five (even though he's quite a bit older), with floppy brown hair and a devastating smile. When he goes out, he usually has his pick of single women, and not just because these women want to get something published in the *New Yorker*. He's smooth and a little sloppy. He sits down next to you and talks to you about politics and asks your opinion. He makes you feel smart. And then, before you know it, he's gone. "Hey, where's Mr. New Yorker?" everyone was asking at eleven o'clock. "He made a phone call," one woman said, "and then he took off on his bike. He was going to meet someone."

The image of Mr. New Yorker, stealing through the night in his tweedy jacket, pumping like mad on his three-speed bike (with fenders to keep his pants from getting dirty), haunted me. I pictured him pulling up to an Upper East Side walkup—or maybe a loft building in SoHo—leaning against the buzzer, and then, panting slightly, wheeling his bike up the stairs. A door would open, and he and his inamorata would be giggling as they tried to figure out where to put the bike. Then they'd fall into a sweaty embrace, no doubt ending up on some futon on the floor.

The Bicycle Boy actually has a long literary-social tradition in New York. The patron saints of Bicycle Boys are white-haired writer George Plimpton, whose bike used to hang upside down above his employees' heads at the *Paris Review* offices, and white-haired *Newsday* columnist Murray Kempton. They've been riding for years and are the inspiration for the next generation of Bicycle Boys, like the aforementioned Mr. New Yorker and scores of young book, magazine, and news-paper editors and writers who insist on traversing Manhattan's physical and romantic landscape as solitary pedalers. Bicycle Boys are a particular breed of New York bachelor: Smart, funny, romantic, lean, quite attractive, they are the stuff that grownup coed dreams are made of. There's something in-credibly, er, charming about a tweedy guy on a bike—espe-cially if he's wearing goofy glasses.

Women tend to feel a mixture of passion and motherly affection. But there's a dark side: Most Bicycle Boys are not married and probably never will be, at least not until they give up their bikes.

WHY JOHN F. KENNEDY JR. IS NOT A BICYCLE BOY

"Riding a bike is not necessarily a power move," said Mr. Eccles. "It's best done by power people like George Plimpton. Otherwise, you have to hide your bike around the corner and surreptitiously take your trousers out of your socks." Bicycle Boys don't ride their bikes for sport, like those silly guys you see riding around and around the park. They ride partly for transportation and, more important, to preserve a literary boyhood. Think of twilight at Oxford, riding over the cobblestones while a woman waits down by the Cherwell River, wearing a flowing dress, clasping a volume of Yeats. That's how Bicycle Boys think of themselves as they pedal Manhattan, dodging cabbies and potholes. While John F. Kennedy Jr. is certainly New York's most famous and sought-after bike-riding bachelor, his rippled athleticism disqualifies him for Bicycle Boydom. Because a Bicycle Boy would rather bike through midtown in a seersucker suit than in shorts and a chest-hugging tee. And Bicycle Boys spurn those skintight bike pants that have cushy foam padding sewn into the butt. Bicycle Boys are not averse to the chastising pain of a hard bike seat—it helps the literature. "I don't own any spandex pants," said Mr. New Yorker, who added that he wears long johns in the winter to keep warm.

Which may be one reason Bicycle Boys, more than their athletic cousins, tend to get physically attacked. The other reason is that they ride at any hour (the later the better—more romantic), in any physical condition, anywhere.

"Drunks roar out of their windows at night to send you into a tailspin," said Mr. Eccles. And worse.

One Halloween, Mr. New Yorker was wearing a British bobby's cape when he rode into a group of twelve year olds who yanked him off his bike. "I said, 'I can't fight all of you at once. I'll fight one of you.' They all stepped back, except for the biggest one. I suddenly realized I didn't want to fight him, either." The whole gang jumped on Mr. New Yorker and began pounding him, until some innocent bystanders started screaming and the gang ran away. "I was lucky," said Mr. New Yorker. "They didn't take my bike, but they did take some records I had in my basket." (Note that Mr. New Yorker was carrying "records," as in vinyl albums, not CDs— another sign of a true Bicycle Boy.)

Mr. Eccles recalled a similar story. "Two days ago, I was riding through Central Park at ten at night, when I was surrounded by a 'wilding' gang on rollerblades. "They were almost children. They tried to capture me in a flank maneuver, but I was able to bicycle away even faster."

But an even bigger danger is sex, as a reporter we'll call Chester found out. Chester doesn't ride his bike as much as he used to because, about a year ago, he had a bad cycling accident after a romantic interlude. He was writing a story on topless dancers when he struck up a friendship with Lola. Maybe Lola fancied herself a Marilyn Monroe to his Arthur Miller. Who knows. All Chester knows is that one evening she called him up and said she was lying around in her bed at Trump Palace, and could he come over. He hopped on his bike and was there in fifteen minutes. They went at it for three hours. Then she said he had to leave because she lived with someone and the guy was coming home. Any minute.

Chester ran out of the building and jumped on his bike, but there was a problem. His legs were so shaky from having sex they started cramping up just as he was going down Murray Hill, and he crashed over the curb and slid across the pavement. "It really hurt," he said. "When your skin is scraped off like that, it's like a first-degree burn." Luckily, his nipple did eventually grow back.

"A BIG STEEL THING BETWEEN MY LEGS"

Riding a bike in Manhattan is indeed perilous sport. If these writers lived out west, maybe they'd carry guns, like something out of Larry McMurtry or Tom McGuane or Cormac McCarthy. But since they live in New York, the Bicycle Boys are more the Clark Kent type. Mild-mannered reporters by day who often have to answer to killer editrixes, they become menaces to society by night. And who can blame them? "You ride through red lights, you ride against the traffic. You can be a felon," said Chester. "I feel like there's a big steel thing between my legs throbbing ahead of me," said one Bicycle Boy, who asked to be unnamed. "I have my hand on my bike right now," said Kip, a literary agent, speaking on the phone from his office. "There's a freedom in being on your bike in the city. You feel like you're floating above the masses. I'm pretty fearless on my bike, in ways that I can't be in the rest of my life. I feel like I'm the best on my bike, the most in tune with myself and the city."

Bicycle boys are particular about their bikes—they don't usually ride souped-up, high-tech, mountain bikes. No Shimano XT derailleurs or elastomer suspension forks for them. More typical is Mr. New Yorker, who rides a polite three-speed, with a basket in back and fenders. The bike should radiate nostalgia. "You have to have a basket for groceries," said Mr. New Yorker, "your computer and work stuff." "My bike is definitely like my dog and my baby," said Kip. "I kind of take care of it and preen it."

But often when Bicycle Boys talk about their bikes, it's hard not to think they are talking about women.

"I love my bike, and you can get attached to a bike," said one B.B., "but the truth is that one bike is very much like another."

"I had one bike that I went completely over the top with," said Kip. "It had an aluminum frame, and I hand-stripped it and polished it. Quite a bit. And then it got stolen. I was emotionally devastated. I couldn't get over it until I got a new bike and really made it beautiful."

Like girlfriends, bikes are always getting stolen in New York. "If you go into a bookstore for ten minutes, you come out and your bike is gone," said Mr. Eccles. This, however, is not necessarily a problem, as Mr. New Yorker pointed out.

"The bike pays for itself in three months if you compare it to subway fare," he said. "One month, if you take taxis."

The bike can also be a useful prop when it comes to meeting women. "It's a good way to start a conversation," said Thad, a writer. "It's also something to fuss with to alleviate your self-consciousness."

And apparently it's a good way to tell whether or not you're going to get laid. "One time, a woman got mad at me when I proposed riding my bike to her house," said Thad. "On the other hand, if a woman says, 'Bring the bike inside,' it's very sexy."

"Whether or not a woman lets you bring your bike into her house is an indication of how well adjusted she is," said Mr. Eccles. "If she's anal-retentive, she won't want the bike anywhere near her stuff."

But sometimes a bike is not just a bike—and women seem to know this. "One is viewed as a suspicious character. You're too mobile and independent," said Mr. Eccles. "And certainly a bit undignified in the end."

"There is something Peter Pan–ish about it," said Kip. "That's part of the reason I don't take it everywhere anymore."

"It implies a certain selfishness," agreed Mr. Eccles. "You can't give anyone a lift. And there's a little too much freedom associated with a man who rides a bike." Mr. Eccles added that, being in his early fifties, there were about ten reasons why he wasn't married, "none of them particularly good ones."

It can also imply a certain cheapness. One woman, an assistant editor at a glossy men's magazine, remembered a date she had with a Bicycle Boy she met at a book signing. After chatting her up, the Bicycle Boy made a date to meet her at a nice steakhouse on the Upper West Side. He showed up, late, on his bike (she was waiting outside, nervously smoking cigarettes), then, after they'd sat down and looked at the menu, he said, "Look, do you mind? I've just realized I'm really in the mood for pizza. You don't care, do you?" He stood up.

"But don't we have to . . . ," she said, glancing at the waiter. He grabbed her arm and hustled her out. "All you had were a few sips of water. I didn't even touch mine. They can't charge you for that."

They went back to her house and ate pizza, and then he made his move. They saw each other a few times after that, but every time, he wanted to come to her house at ten at night and eat takeout food. She finally ditched him and went out with a banker.

THE CROTCH PROBLEM

Bicycle Boys often make the mistake of trying to turn their girlfriends into Bicycle Girls. Joanna, a woman who grew up on Fifth Avenue and now works as an interior designer, actually married a Bicycle Boy. "We both rode bikes," she said, "so at first it wasn't a problem. But I noticed something was kind of wrong when he gave me a bicycle seat for my birthday. Then, for Christmas, he gave me a bike rack to put on the car. When we got divorced, he took the bike rack back and kept it for himself. Can you believe that?"

"Boys on bikes? God, no," said Magda, the novelist. "Can you imagine what a stinky crotch they have? No, thank you. I've been mowed down too many times by men on bikes. They're all kamikaze selfish pricks. If they have sex the way they ride their bikes, thank you, but speed is not important."

"Women don't think riding a bike is sexy," said Thad. "They think it's infantile. But at some point, you decide that you can't go through life giving women a false impression of who you are."

10

Downtown Babes Meet Old Greenwich Gals

The pilgrimage to the newly suburbanized friend is one that most Manhattan women have made, and few truly enjoyed. In fact, most come back to the city in an emotional state somewhere between giddy and destroyed. Here follows one such tale.

Jolie Bernard used to be an agent who handled rock bands at International Creative Management. Five years ago, when she wasn't stomping the globe in her cowboy boots, hanging out with rock stars and sometimes sleeping with them, she lived in New York, in a one-bedroom apartment decorated with black leather couches and a giant stereo system. She had long blond hair and a tight little body with big tits, and when she came home she had a million messages on her answering machine, and when she went out, she had money and drugs in her purse. She was kind of famous.

And then something happened. No one thought it would, but it did, which just goes to show that you can never tell about these things. She turned thirty-five and she met this investment banker who worked for Salomon Brothers, and before you knew it, they were married, she was pregnant, and they were moving to Greenwich.

"Nothing will change," she said. "We'll still get together all the time and you can come to visit us and we'll have barbecues in the summer."

We all said, Yeah, yeah, yeah.

Two years went by. We heard she'd had one rug rat, and then another. We could never remember their names or if they were boys or girls.

"Hey, how's Jolie?" I would ask Miranda, who was at one time Jolie's best friend.

"Dunno," Miranda would say. "Every time I call her, she can't talk. The sprinkler man is coming, or she caught the nanny smoking pot in the laundry room, or one of the kids is screaming."

"Horrible. Just horrible," we would say, and then we would forget about it.

And then, a month ago, the inevitable happened: Little white invitations bordered with tiny purple flowers arrived, summoning four of Jolie's city friends to a bridal shower she was hosting at her house. It was being held on a Saturday at one P.M.—only, as Miranda pointed out, the most inconvenient time and the last thing you want to be doing with your Saturday afternoon. Schlepping to Connecticut.

"Jolie called and begged me," Miranda said. "She said she wanted some of her city friends to come so it wouldn't be too boring."

"The kiss of death," I said.

Still, the four women did agree to go—Miranda, thirty-two, a cable exec; Sarah, thirty-eight, who ran her own PR company; Carrie, thirty-four, some sort of journalist; and Belle, thiry-four, a banker and the only married woman of the group.

OLD GREENWICH, NEW ENEMIES

Of course, Saturday was the most beautiful day of the year so far. Sunny, seventy degrees. When they met up at Grand Central, everyone began complaining immediately about having to be stuck inside Jolie's house on the most beautiful day of the year, even though, being dyed-in-the-wool city dwellers, none of them ever went outside if they could possibly avoid it.

The trouble began on the train. As usual, Carrie had gone to bed at four in the morning, and she was terribly hung over and kept thinking she was going to puke. Belle got into an argument with the woman in front of her, whose kid kept sticking its head over the top of the seat and sticking his tongue out at her.

Then Sarah revealed that Jolie was in A.A.—had been for three months—which meant there might not be cocktails at the shower.

Carrie and Miranda immediately decided they would get off the train at the next stop and go back to the city, but Belle and Sarah wouldn't let them; and then Sarah told Carrie that she should probably join A.A. herself.

The train stopped in Old Greenwich, and the four women crammed into the back seat of a white and green cab.

"Why are we doing this?" Sarah asked.

"Because we have to," Carrie said.

"They just better not have any trendy gardening tools lying around," said Miranda. "If I see gardening tools, I'm going to scream."

"If I see kids, I'm going to scream."

"Look. Grass. Trees. Breathe in the aroma of freshly mown grass," said Carrie, who had mysteriously begun to feel better. Everyone looked at her suspiciously.

The cab pulled up in front of a white, Colonial-style house whose value had obviously been increased by the addition of a pointy slate roof and balconies off the second floor. The lawn was very green, and the trees that dotted the yard had borders of pink flowers around their bases.

"Oh, what a cute puppy," Carrie said, as a golden retriever raced barking across the lawn. But as the dog reached the edge of the yard, it was suddenly jerked back, as if yanked by an invisible rope.

Miranda lit up a blue Dunhill. "Invisible electric fencing," she said. "They all have it. And I bet you anything we're going to have to hear about it."

For a moment, the four women stood in the driveway, staring at the dog, who was now sitting, subdued but valiantly wagging its tail, in the middle of the yard.

"Can we go back to the city now, please?" Sarah asked.

Inside the house, half a dozen women were already sitting in the living room, legs crossed, balancing cups of coffee and tea on their knees. A spread was laid out: cucumber sandwiches, quesadillas with salsa. Sitting off to one side, unopened, untouched, was a big bottle of white wine, its sides covered in a film of moisture. The bride-to-be, Lucy, looked somewhat terrified at the city women's arrival.

There were introductions all around.

A woman named Brigid Chalmers, Hermes from head to toe, was sipping what looked like a bloody mary. "You guys are late. Jolie thought maybe you weren't coming," she said, with that particular breezy nastiness that only women can show to one another.

"Well, the train schedule," Sarah shrugged apologetically.

"Excuse me, but do we know you?" Miranda whispered in Carrie's ear. That meant as far as Miranda was concerned, it was war with Brigid from now on.

"Is that a bloody mary?" Carrie asked.

Brigid and one of the other women exchanged glances. "Actually, it's a virgin mary," she said. Her eyes flickered in Jolie's direction for a second. "I did all that stuff for years. All that drinking and partying. And then, I don't know, it just gets boring. You move on to more important things."

"The only important thing to me right now is vodka," Carrie said, putting her hands to her head. "I've got the worst hangover. If I don't get some vodka . . ."

"Raleigh!" said one of the women on the couch, bending

around to peer into one of the other rooms. "Raleigh! Go outside and play."

Miranda leaned over to Carrie: "Is she talking to her dog or her kid?"

"MARRIED SEX"

Miranda turned to Brigid. "So tell me, Brigid," she said. "What exactly is it that you do?"

Brigid opened her mouth and neatly inserted a quesadilla triangle. "I work at home. I've got my own consulting firm."

"I see," Miranda said, nodding. "And what do you consult on?"

"Computers."

"She's our sort of neighborhood Bill Gates," said another woman, named Marguerite, drinking Evian from a wine goblet. "Whenever we have a computer problem, we call Brigid, and she can fix it."

"That's so important when you have a computer," Belle said. "Computers can be so tricky. Especially if you don't use one every day." She smiled. "And what about you, Marguerite? Do you have children?"

Marguerite blushed slightly and looked away. "One," she said a little wistfully. "One beautiful little angel. Of course, he's not so little anymore. He's eight, he's in that real-boy stage. But we're trying for another."

"Margie's on that in-vitro trail," Jolie said, and then, addressing the room, added, "I'm so glad I got my two over with early."

Unfortunately, Carrie chose that moment to emerge from the kitchen sipping on a large glass of vodka with two ice cubes floating on the top. "Speaking of rug rats," she said, "Belle's husband wants her to get preggers, but she doesn't want to. So she went to a drug store, bought one of those test kits that tell you when you're ovulating, and the woman behind the counter was like, 'Good luck!' And Belle was like, 'No, no, you don't understand. I'm going to use this so I know when not to have sex.' Isn't that hysterical?"

"I can't possibly be pregnant during the summer," Belle said. "I wouldn't want to be seen in a bathing suit."

Brigid yanked the conversation back. "And what do you do, Miranda?" she asked. "You live in the city, don't you?"

"Well, actually, I'm the executive director at a cable company."

"Oh, I love cable," said a woman named Rita, who was wearing three heavy gold necklaces and sporting a twelve-carat sapphire engagement ring next to a sapphire-encrusted wedding band.

"Yes," Belle said, smiling sweetly. "We think of Miranda as our own little Bob Pittman. He started MTV, you know."

"Oh, I know," said Rita. "My husband is at CBS. I should tell him I met you, Miranda. I'm sure he'd—in fact, I was his assistant! Until everyone found out we were seeing each other. Especially since he was married at the time." She and the other Connecticut women exchanged glances.

Carrie plunked down next to Rita, accidentally sloshing her with some vodka.

"So sorry," she said. "I'm so damn clumsy today. Napkin?"

"That's okay," Rita said.

"It's just so fascinating," Carrie said. "Getting a married man. I would never be able to pull it off. I'd probably end up becoming best friends with his wife."

"That's why there are courses at the Learning Annex," Sarah said dryly.

"Yeah, but I don't want to take courses with a bunch of losers," Carrie said.

"I know a lot of people who have taken courses at the Learning Annex. And they're pretty good," Brigid said.

"What was our favorite?" Rita asked. "The S&M course. How to be a dominatrix."

"Well, whipping is just about the only way I can keep my husband awake," Brigid said. "Married sex."

Lucy laughed gamely.

SUBURBAN SURPRISE: BIDET

Carrie stood up and yawned. "Does anyone know where the bathroom is?"

Carrie did not go to the bathroom. Nor was she as drunk as she appeared to be. Instead, she tiptoed up the stairs, carpeted with an oriental runner, and thought that if she were Jolie, she would probably know what kind of oriental rug it was because that was the kind of stuff you were supposed to know if you were married to a rich banker and making him a home in the suburbs.

She went into Jolie's bedroom. There was a thick white carpet on the floor and photographs everywhere in silver frames, some professional-looking shots of Jolie in a bathing suit, her long blond hair swinging over her shoulders.

Carrie stared at those photographs for a long time. What was it like to be Jolie? How did it happen? How did you find someone who fell in love with you and gave you all this? She was thirty-four and she'd never even come close, and there was a good chance she never would.

And this was the kind of life she'd grown up believing she could have, simply because she wanted it. But the men you wanted didn't want it, or you; and the men who did want it were too boring. She went into the bathroom. Floor-to-ceiling black marble. A bidet. Maybe suburban husbands wouldn't play ball unless their wives were just-washed, unlike guys in the city. Then she almost screamed.

There was a fourteen-by-seventeen color photograph of Jolie, Demi Moore–style, naked save for a skimpy negligee that was open in the front to reveal humongous tits and a huge belly. Jolie was staring proudly into the camera, her hand resting just above her belly button, which had been pushed straight out like a little stem. Carrie flushed the toilet and ran breathless down the stairs.

"We're opening presents," Brigid scolded.

Carrie sat down in a chair next to Miranda. "What's your problem?" Miranda asked.

"Photograph. In the master bathroom. Check it out," Carrie said.

"Excuse me," Miranda said, leaving the room.

"What are you two doing?" Jolie asked.

"Nothing," Carrie said. She looked at the bride-to-be, who was holding up a pair of red silk, crotchless panties bordered in black lace. Everyone was laughing. Which is what you do at showers.

"I'M SHAKING"

"Could you believe the photograph?" Miranda asked. They were rocking gently on the train back to the city.

"If I ever get pregnant," Belle said, "I'm going to stay inside for nine months. I will see no one."

"I think I could get into it," Sarah said moodily, staring out the window. "They've got houses and cars and nannies. Their lives look so manageable. I'm jealous."

"What do they do all day? That's what I want to know," Miranda said.

"They don't even have sex," Carrie said. She was thinking about her new boyfriend, Mr. Big. Right now, things were great, but after a year, or two years—if it even lasted that long—then what happened?

"You wouldn't believe the story I heard about Brigid," Belle said. "While you guys were upstairs, Jolie pulled me into the kitchen. 'Be nice to Brigid,' she said. 'She just found her husband, Tad, in flagrante with another woman.'"

The other woman was Brigid's next door neighbor, Susan. Susan and Tad both worked in the city and for the last year had carpooled to and from the train each day. When Brigid found them, it was ten in the evening and they were both drunk in the car, parked at the cul-de-sac at the end of the street. Brigid had been out walking the dog.

She yanked open the car door and tapped Tad on his naked bum. "Wheaton has the flu and wants to say good night to his daddy," she said, then went back inside.

For the next week, she continued to ignore the situation, while Tad became more and more agitated, sometimes calling her ten times a day from his office. Every time he tried to bring it up, she brought up something about their two children. Finally, on Saturday night, when Tad was getting stoned and mixing up margaritas on the deck, she told him. "I'm pregnant again. Three months. So we shouldn't have to worry about a miscarriage this time. Aren't you happy, dear?" Then she took the pitcher of margaritas and poured it over his head.

"Typical," Carrie said, cleaning under her fingernails with the edge of a matchbook.

"I'm just so happy I can trust my husband," Belle said.

"I'm shaking," Miranda said. They saw the city, dusky and brown, looming up as the train went over a bridge. "I need a drink. Anyone coming?"

After three cocktails at Ici, Carrie called Mr. Big.

"Yo, yo," he said. "What up."

"It was awful," she giggled. "You know how much I hate those kinds of things. All they talked about was babies and private schools and how this friend of theirs got blackballed from the country club and how one of their nannies crashed a new Mercedes."

She could hear Mr. Big puffing away on his cigar. "Don't worry, kid. You'll get used to it," he said.

"I don't think so," she said.

She turned and looked back to their table. Miranda had shanghaied two guys from another table, one of whom was already in deep conversation with Sarah.

"Gimme shelter—in Bowery Bar," she said, and hung up.

11

Babes Flee Land of Wives for Night of Topless Fun

Bad things can happen to city women when they come back from visiting their newly married-with-children friends in the suburbs.

The morning after Carrie, Miranda, Belle, and Sarah returned from a bridal shower in Greenwich, there were phone calls.

Sarah had broken her ankle rollerblading at four in the morning. Miranda had had sex with some guy in a closet at a party, and they didn't use condoms. Carrie had done something so ridiculous she was sure her short relationship with Mr. Big was over. And no one could find Belle.

THE BOLD FELLOW

Miranda hadn't meant to go nuts at the party, to go into what she calls "my Glenn Close imitation."

"I was just going to go home and get a good night's sleep and wake up and work on Sunday." That was the great thing about not being married, not having kids, being alone. You could work on Sunday.

But Sarah made her go to the party. "There could be good contacts there," Sarah had said. Sarah, with her own PR company, was constantly on the lookout for "contacts," which could also translate to "dates." The party was on East 64th Street. Some rich old guy's town house. Women in their thirties wearing black dresses and all with practically the same color blond hair. That type of woman always went to parties at rich old guys' houses, and they always brought their girl-friends, so there were squadrons of these women looking for men and pretending not to.

Sarah disappeared into the throng. Miranda was left standing by the bar. She had dark, wavy hair, and she was wearing leggings with the boot part sewn in, so she stuck out.

Two girls walked by her, and Miranda—maybe she is a little paranoid—swore that one of them said, "That's that girl, Miranda Hobbes. She's a total bitch."

So Miranda said, out loud, but so no one could hear, "That's right, I am a real bitch, honey, but thank God I'm not like you." Then she remembered how at the end of the long afternoon in the suburbs, the low-fat carrot cake with low-fat cream cheese frosting had been served with tiny sterling forks with prongs so sharp they could break the skin.

A man came up to her. Expensively tailored suit. Okay, he wasn't exactly a man because he was only about thirty-five. But he was trying. She was making the bartender give her a double vodka tonic, and the man said, "Thirsty, eh?"

"No. What I really want is a steak. Okay?"

"I will get you one," the man said, and it turned out he had a French accent.

"I will let you know," she said, and tried to walk away. She didn't want to have anything to do with the party. She was tired of feeling like she didn't fit in, but she didn't want to go home, either, because she was tired of being lonely and she was a little drunk.

"My name is Guy," he said. "I own a gallery on 79th Street."

She sighed and said, "Of course you do."

"Perhaps you have heard of it."

"Listen, Guy . . .," she said.

"Yes?" he asked eagerly.

"Can you touch your asshole with your dick?"

Guy smiled slyly. He moved closer. Put his hand on her shoulder. "But of course."

"Then I suggest you go fuck yourself."

"A come-on!" Guy said, and Miranda wondered if he was really that stupid, or if he just seemed stupid because he was French. He grabbed her hand and began pulling her up the stairs; she went along because she figured that any guy who could keep his cool after being insulted couldn't be that bad. They ended up in the rich old guy's bedroom, which had a red silk cover on the bed, and then this Guy character had some cocaine. And then, somehow, they ended up kissing. People kept coming in and out of the bedroom.

For some reason, they went into the walk-in closet. Old pine paneling, racks for jackets and trousers, shelves for cashmere sweaters and shoes. Miranda checked the labels: Savile Row—boring. Then she turned around, and Guy was standing right there. Then there was the groping. The leggings came down. Out popped the bold fellow.

"How big?" Carrie asked her on the phone.

"Big. And French," Miranda said. (How could she?)

And then, afterward, he said, "Hey, darling, you'd better not tell my girlfriend." As he stuck his tongue in her mouth one final time.

It all came spilling out: the girlfriend whom he'd lived with for two years, and they were engaged, sort of, but he really didn't know if he wanted to get married, but she was living with him, so what could he do?

And then it was Glenn Close without the rabbit.

The next day, Guy tracked down Miranda's number and called her, wanting to see her again. "And this is what we have to choose from," Miranda said.

NEWBERT GETS WORRIED

At noon, Belle's husband, Newbert, called Carrie to see if she'd seen Belle.

"If she were dead, I'd know about it," Carrie said.

A ROLLERBLADE INGENUE

Then there was Sarah, who, according to Miranda, went rollerblading in her basement at four A.M. Drunk. Thirty-eight years old. A grown woman clinging to the role of ingenue. Is there anything less attractive? I don't think so.

But what is Sarah supposed to do? She is 38, and she's not married, and she'd like to be with someone. And men, as we know from this column, are attracted to youth. Even the women at the bridal shower, older than Sarah now, were younger than she is when they got married. It may not be an option for her anymore. So she rollerblades with a twenty-five year old in her basement. Instead of having sex with him. He wants to; she is afraid he'll think her body's too old.

"Oh hi-i-i," Sarah says, when Carrie calls her in the afternoon. She's laid up on the couch in her tiny but perfect one-bedroom apartment in a high-rise just west of Second Avenue. "Oh I'm fi-i-i-ne. Can you believe it?" she sounds unnaturally cheerful. "Just a little broken ankle. And the cutest doctors in the emergency room. And Luke with me the whole time."

"Luke?"

"Lucas really. The cutest guy. My little friend." She's giggling. A horrifying sound.

"Where did you get the rollerblades?"

"Oh, he came on them. To the party. Isn't that cute?"

The cast comes off in six weeks. In the meantime, Sarah will have to hobble around, running her PR business as best she can. She has no disability insurance. The business runs on a shoestring.

Is this better or worse than being married and living in the suburbs? Better or worse?

Who can tell.

BELLE AT THE CARLYLE

Belle calls from the Carlyle. Mentions something about a wide receiver from the Miami Dolphins. At Frederick's. Mentions something about her husband, Newbert, and some spaghetti sauce. "I make great spaghetti sauce," she says. "I'm a great wife." Carrie agrees.

Anyway, after she got home from the bridal shower, she and Newbert had a fight. Belle ran away, went to Frederick's, the nightclub. The wide receiver was at Frederick's. He kept telling her that her husband didn't love her enough. "He does. You don't understand," she said. "I'd love you more," he said. She laughed, ran away again, booked herself a suite in the Carlyle. She says, "Cocktails are being served. Now."

She says she thinks maybe Newbert is upset because he's just sent out his novel. She thinks maybe Newbert is upset because she doesn't want to have kids. Not until he sells his novel. When she gets pregnant, it will all be over. So better to have a good time now.

ALL ROADS LEAD TO BABY DOLL

After the bridal shower, and after checking in on the phone with her new boyfriend, Mr. Big, Carrie went to Bowery Bar. Samantha Jones, the fortyish movie producer was there. Carrie's best friend. Sometimes.

Barkley, the twenty-five-year-old up-and-coming artist and model chaser, had inserted himself at Samantha's table.

"I'd love it if you'd stop by my loft sometime," Barkley said, flipping his blond hair out of his eyes.

Samantha was smoking a Cuban cigar. She took a drag and blew the thick smoke in Barkley's face. "I'll bet you would. But what makes you think I'd like your little paintings."

"Well, you don't have to like my paintings," Barkley said. "You could just like me."

Samantha grinned evilly. "I don't bother with men under thirty-five. They're not experienced enough for my tastes."

"Try me," Barkley said. "If not, at least buy me a drink."

"We're leaving," Samantha said. "We have to find a new hangout."

They found one. The Baby Doll Lounge. Strip joint in TriBeCa. They couldn't shake Barkley, so they let him come along. It might be good to have a guy with them at a topless bar. Plus, he had smoke. They smoked in the cab, and when they got out at the Baby Doll Lounge, Sam grabbed Carrie's arm (Sam almost never did stuff like that) and said, "I really want to know about Mr. Big. I'm not sure he's the right man for you."

Carrie had to think about whether she wanted to answer or not, because it was always like this between her and Sam. Just when she was happy with a man, Sam would come along and insert those doubts, like driving a crowbar between two pieces of wood. She said, "I don't know. I think I'm crazy about him."

Sam said, "But does he really know how great you are? How great I think you are?"

Carrie thought, "Someday, Sam and I will sleep with the same man at once, but not tonight."

The bartender, a woman, came over and said, "It's so nice to see women in here again," and began pouring them free drinks. That was always a problem. Then Barkley was trying to have a discussion. About how he really wanted to be a director and how that was what all the artists were doing anyway, so why shouldn't he just skip the boring artist part and start directing?

Two girls were dancing on the stage. They looked like real women, and they didn't look so good—small saggy breasts and big bottoms. By now, Barkley was screaming, "But I'm better than David Salle! I'm a fucking genius!"

"Oh, yeah? Says who?" Sam screamed back.

"We're all fucking geniuses," Carrie said. Then she went to the bathroom.

You had to walk through a tiny slot in between the two stages, and then downstairs. The bathroom had a gray wooden door that wouldn't shut properly, and broken tiles. She thought about Greenwich. Marriage. Kids.

"I'm not ready," she thought.

She went upstairs, and she took her clothes off and got up on the stage and started to dance. Samantha was staring at her, laughing, but by the time the bartender came over and politely told her to get down, Sam wasn't laughing anymore.

The next morning, Mr. Big called at eight A.M. He was going to play golf. He sounded tense. "When did you get home?" he asked. "What did you do?"

"Not much," she said. "Went to Bowery. And then this other place. The Baby Doll Lounge."

"Oh yeah? Do anything special there?"

"Had too much to drink." She laughed.

"Nothing else you want to tell me?"

"No, not really," Carrie said in the little-girl voice she used when she wanted to soothe him. "What about you?"

"I got a phone call this morning," he said. "Someone said they saw you dancing topless at the Baby Doll Lounge."

"Oh. Really?" she said. "How did they know it was me?"

"They knew."

"Are you mad?"

"Why didn't you tell me?" he asked.

"Are you mad?"

"I'm mad you didn't tell me. How can you have a relationship if you can't be honest?"

"But how do I know I can trust you?" she asked.

"Believe me," he said. "I'm the one person you can trust." And he hung up.

Carrie took all their pictures from Jamaica (how happy they looked, just discovering each other), and cut out the ones of

Mr. Big smoking his cigar. She thought about what it was like sleeping with him, how she would sleep curled around his back.

She wanted to take the pictures and glue them to a piece of construction paper and write "Portrait of Mr. Big with His Cigar," across the top and then, "I miss you," with lots of kisses at the bottom.

She stared at the pictures for a long time. And then she did nothing.

12

Skipper and Mr. Marvelous
Seek Hot Sex in
Southampton Hedges

Maybe it's just the indisputable fact that most people really do look better with a tan. Or maybe it's proof that the sex drive is stronger than ambition, even for New Yorkers. In any case, there is something about the Hamptons that lends itself to meaningless sexual encounters, the kind of embarrassingly brief couplings that most people don't necessarily want to acknowledge in the morning.

Call it a combination of skin (the topless women on Media Beach), geography (it takes sooooo long to drive from Southampton to East Hampton, especially if it's four in the morning), and topography (all those high hedges where couples can hide).

But figuring out how to work all those elements to one's advantage, especially if you're a man, can take some finesse. And youth is not necessarily an advantage. You have to know the ropes and how to get out of them gracefully afterward. Otherwise, you'll end up with something, but it might not be what you expected.

Here's a cautionary tale about three hopeful bachelors in the Hamptons during Fourth of July weekend.

But first, meet our contestants.

Bachelor No. 1: Skipper Johnson, twenty-five. Preppy. Entertainment law. Boy wonder. Plans to run one of the big studios someday, which he says will be in New York. Beach toys: small Mercedes, Brooks Brothers clothing ("I have a Brooks Brothers body"), and cellular phone, of which he makes constant use. Recently, friends complained that Skipper spent two hours in the parking lot at the beach, on the phone, doing a deal. "It's such a waste of time going to the beach," Skipper says. "Besides, I don't like getting sandy." Is worried about his recent lack of sexual success. "Do women think I'm gay?" he asks, earnestly.

Bachelor No. 2: Mr. Marvelous, sixty-five, says he's sixty. Square jaw, silver hair, bright blue eyes, athletic—all parts work on demand. Married (and divorced) five times. Twelve kids—wives number two, three, and four all good friends. Buddies wonder what his secret is. Beach toys: none. But can talk about penthouse apartment on Park Avenue, house in Bedford, apartment in Palm Beach. Staying with friends for the weekend on Further Lane in East Hampton. Considering buying a place.

Bachelor No. 3: Stanford Blatch, thirty-seven. Screenwriter. The next Joe Eszterhas. Gay but prefers straight guys. Long, dark, curly hair; refuses to cut it or put it in a ponytail. Will probably get married and have kids someday. Stays in Grandmother's house on Halsey Neck Lane in Southampton; Grandma lives in Palm Beach. Beach toys: doesn't drive, so convinces family chauffeur to come out on weekends to drive him around. Best beach toy: has known everybody worth knowing since he was a child, so he doesn't have to prove it.

SKIPPER'S COLD SHOWER

Friday night. Skipper Johnson drives out to Southampton, where he has arranged to meet friends at Basilico: four women, all in their late twenties, who work at Ralph Lauren, and who, to the naked eye, are indistinguishable from one another. Skipper finds their bland prettiness comforting, as well as the fact that there's a small herd of them. It means that he doesn't have the burden of trying to keep one of them entertained for the evening.

They drink Pine Hamptons at the bar. Skipper pays. At eleven o'clock, they go to M-80. There's a crowd outside, but Skipper knows the doorman. They drink cocktails out of plastic cups. Skipper runs into some friends—the modelizers George and Charlie. "I've got twelve girls staying at my place this weekend," George boasts to Skipper. George knows that Skipper is dying to come over, so he purposely doesn't invite him. Two of the models begin throwing cocktails at each other, laughing.

At two A.M., one of the girls gets sick in the bushes. Skipper offers to drive them home: a ranch house just before you get to the good part of Southampton. They have a case of beer in the refrigerator, nothing else. Skipper goes into a bedroom and sits on the bed with one of the girls and sips a beer. He lies down and closes his eyes, slipping his arm around the girl's waist. "I'm too drunk to drive home," he says in a puppy dog voice.

"I'm going to sleep," the girl says.

"Oh, please let me stay. We'll just sleep. I promise," Skipper says.

"Okay. But you have to sleep on top of the bed. With your clothes on."

Skipper complies. He falls asleep and begins snoring. Sometime in the middle of the night, the girl kicks him out to the couch.

Saturday morning. Skipper drives toward his house in East Hampton and decides to stop off to visit his friends Carrie and Mr. Big in Bridgehampton. Mr. Big is shirtless in the backyard, smoking a cigar and watering the plants around the pool. "I'm on vacation," he says.

"What are you doing? Don't you have a gardener?" Skipper asks. Carrie is smoking cigarettes and reading the *New York Post*. "He is the gardener. He washes cars, too."

Skipper strips down to his boxer shorts and dives in the water like a cartoon character, with his knees bent at right angles sticking out to the sides. When he comes up for air, Mr. Big says, "Now I know why you can't get laid."

"What am I supposed to do?" Skipper asks.

"Have a cigar," says Mr. Big.

MR. BLATCH IN LOVE

Saturday, Halsey Neck Lane. Stanford Blatch is sitting by the pool, talking on the phone and watching his brother's girl-friend, whom he hates, trying to read his *New York Observer*. He's talking in an especially loud voice in the hope that she might go away. "But you have to come out," he says into the phone. "It's ridiculous. What are you going to do? Sit in the city all weekend and work? Get on the seaplane. I'll pay.

"Well, bring the manuscripts. You agents, you work too damn hard. Of course there's plenty of room. I have the whole upstairs."

Stanford hangs up. He walks over to his brother's girlfriend. "Do you know Robert Morriskin?" When the girl looks at him blankly, he says, "I didn't think so. He's the hottest up-and-coming literary agent. He's adorable."

"Is he a writer?" she asks.

SKIPPER BLOWS IT

Saturday night. Skipper goes to a barbecue at the home of his friends the Rappaports, a young couple who always seem to be on the verge of divorce. He gets drunk again and tries the "drinking beer and lying on the bed" trick again with a girl named Cindy. It seems to be working, until he mentions that he thinks Jim Carrey is a genius.

"You know, I have a boyfriend," she says.

Sunday. Mr. Marvelous calls his friends, tells them he's sick of Bedford and is coming out in his Ferrari.

Stanford Blatch is sitting out by the pool in a paisley Armani cabana suit. A short-sleeved jacket and tight-fitting trunks.

He's on the phone again to Robert Morriskin. "Why don't you come out tonight? There's a great party. There aren't that many great parties out here anymore, you know? Are you bringing a date? Bring a girl if you want. I don't care."

SOMETHING AMAZING HAPPENS

Sunday night. Coerte Felske's book party at Ted Fields's house. Skipper hasn't been invited, which pisses him off. Nevertheless, he has arranged to go to the party by offering to drive Stanford Blatch, whom he knows vaguely and who is invited everywhere, to the party.

The party is outside. Skipper notices that a young woman named Margaret is paying a lot of attention to him. Margaret is short, with dark hair and large breasts, pretty—but not Skipper's type. Works in public relations. Skipper and Margaret decide they have to go to the bathroom, which means walking along a torchlit path snaking behind some bushes to the porta-potties. They head for some hedges. They start kissing. And then something amazing happens.

"I just really want to do this," Margaret says, and she kneels down and unzips his pants. Skipper is astounded. The whole act takes less than two minutes.

"You're going to give me a ride home, aren't you?" Margaret says, nudging him.

"I can't," he says. "I promised I would give Stanford a ride home, and you live in the opposite direction."

OH, MR. MARVELOUS!

Further Lane. Mr. Marvelous from Bedford arrives just in time for dinner. His host, Charlie, has been divorced for five years. He's invited some men and some women in their thirties to early forties. Mr. Marvelous sits next to a woman named Sabrina: thirty-two, breasts spilling out of a black Donna Karan tank top. Mr. Marvelous gets her drinks, is sympathetic about her ex-husband. At eleven o'clock, Sabrina says they have to go to Stephen's Talk House in Amagansett to meet some friends. Mr. Marvelous offers to drive her car, she might be a little drunk. They end up at Sabrina's house at three in the morning.

When he walks in, her girlfriend says, "If you've got any kinky ideas in your head, you can just forget them right now." She lies down on the couch and turns out the light.

Later, about five in the morning, Mr. Marvelous begins feeling claustrophobic. Sabrina's house is tiny. He can hear her friend snoring on the couch just outside the bedroom door. "I'm going out of my mind," he thinks.

Monday. Mr. Marvelous calls Sabrina, whom he just left an hour before. Her machine is on. "Do you want to come to the beach?" He goes to Media Beach, meets Carrie and Mr. Big. Then he spots an attractive blond with a cocker spaniel. He walks up to her and starts playing with her dog. They get into a conversation. He thinks he's getting somewhere when her boyfriend walks up. A big, hulking guy with an overdeveloped chest and short legs. Mr. Marvelous returns to his towel. Samantha Jones is there, sitting with Carrie and Mr. Big.

The girl and her boyfriend walk up the beach. When the blond passes Mr. Marvelous, she turns and waves.

"See? I told you she was interested. Really interested," Mr. Marvelous says.

"In you?" Samantha asks. She laughs meanly.

CELLULAR BREAKDOWN

Skipper is playing tennis when he hears his cellular phone ringing.

"Hi, honey," Margaret says. "Just wondering what you're doing."

"I'm in the middle of a tennis game," Skipper says.

"Wanna come over after? I'd love to cook you dinner over here."

"Uh, I can't."

"What do you mean, you can't?"

"I mean, I don't know what I'm doing yet. I told some other people I would go over to their house for dinner."

"So we'll go together."

Skipper lowers his voice. "I don't think I can do that. It's kind of business, you know what I mean?"

"My little mogul," Margaret says.

Robert Morriskin finally arrives by seaplane. Stanford is a little pissed he didn't come the day before, so he sends the chauffeur in the old Ford station wagon to pick him up instead of the Mercedes.

Mr. Marvelous returns from the beach. Sabrina called. He calls her back immediately but gets her machine.

"IS IT ELLE?"

Monday evening. Carrie, Mr. Big, and Mr. Marvelous are on their way to a cocktail party. Mr. Marvelous drives his big Mercedes slowly up Mecox Lane, past the horse farms. The sun is beginning to go down, and the grass has a particular green calmness. There's a little hill, and when the car comes over the top, there's a woman awkwardly rollerblading. She's wearing a tight white T-shirt and tiny black shorts. She has long dark hair tied up in a ponytail, but it's her legs that get you.

"I'm in love," Mr. Marvelous says. When she turns off down a side road, he drives the car straight on, but then stops and puts his hands on top of the steering wheel. "I'm going back."

Carrie tries to give Mr. Big a look, but he ignores her. He is laughing, going along with it all.

Mr. Marvelous speeds up the road after the girl. "Look at her. She doesn't even know how to rollerblade. She's going to get hurt." They pass the girl, and Mr. Big says, "Is it Elle? She looks like Elle."

Carrie's sitting in the back seat, smoking a cigarette. "Too young for Elle," she says.

Mr. Big rolls down his window and says, "Hi."

The girl comes up to the car. "Hi," she says smiling, then looks confused. "Do I know you?"

"I don't know," says Mr. Marvelous, leaning across the seat. "I'm Mr. Marvelous."

"I'm Audrey," says the girl. She looks at Mr. Big. "You look like someone I know."

Mr. Marvelous hops out of the car. "Do you know how to stop? You've got to know how to stop. Rollerblading can be dangerous."

The girl is laughing. "Here's what you do," Mr. Marvelous says, demonstrating by squatting down with one foot in front of him and sticking his arms straight out.

"Thank you," the girl says. She begins to skate away. "Are you a model?" Mr. Marvelous says.

"No," she says, over her shoulder. "No, I'm a student."

Mr. Marvelous gets back in the car. "She had a ring on her finger. What's her husband doing letting her go rollerblading by herself? I would have asked her to marry me. She was that beautiful. Did you see her? What was her name? Audrey. Her name was Audrey. Kind of old-fashioned, huh?"

THE BOY IN BLUE CHINTZ

Stanford has arranged a dinner at Della Femina's for Robert. Afterward, they all go back to the house on Halsey Neck and smoke pot. At two in the morning, Robert begs off, saying he's got to plow through that pile of manuscripts in the morning. Stanford walks him to his room, which is decorated in traditional Southampton chintz. "I've always loved this room," Stanford says. "You can't get this blue chintz anymore. I hope you won't be too hot. I still think it's best to sleep without the covers in the summer. We used to do that when we were kids. Before my grandmother discovered air conditioning."

Stanford sits down in an armchair as Robert gets undressed. Robert doesn't seem to mind, and Stanford keeps up a patter of chitchat. Robert gets into bed and closes his eyes. "Tired?" Stanford says. He walks to the bed and looks down at Robert, whose eyes are closed. "Are you sleeping?"

INDEPENDENCE DAY

Tuesday, Fourth of July. The cellular phone: It's Margaret. "Hi, honey. Everybody's going back early, and I don't want to. When are you going back? Can I get a ride?"

"I'm not going back until tomorrow morning," Skipper says.

"Oh. Well, I could go back tomorrow morning. I'll call my office."

"Sure," says Skipper, unhappily.

"Don't you just love the end of the weekend when everyone's left and you're still out here? Let's go to dinner."

"I don't think I can. I promised some friends . . . "

"No problem," Margaret says lightly. "We'll definitely see each other next weekend. We can plan it in the car tomorrow morning."

Tuesday, early evening. Mr. Marvelous turns his Mercedes into the road where he last saw Audrey. He gets out, opens the trunk, and after a certain amount of struggle, puts on a pair of rollerblades. He takes a couple of turns up and down the road. Then he leans against the side of his car and waits.

13

Tales of the Pretty

On a recent afternoon, four women met at an Upper East Side restaurant to discuss what it's like to be an extremely beautiful young woman in New York City. About what it's like to be sought after, paid for, bothered, envied, misunderstood, and just plain gorgeous—all before the age of twenty-five.

Camilla was the first to arrive. Five feet ten, pale white skin, big lips, round cheekbones, tiny nose—Camilla is twenty-five but says she "feels old." She began modeling at sixteen. When I first met her, months ago downtown, she was doing her duty as a "date" to a well-known television producer, which meant she was smiling and speaking back when someone asked her a question. Other than that, she was making very little effort, except to occasionally light her own cigarettes.

Women like Camilla don't need to make much effort, especially with men. While many women would have killed to have a date with Scotty, the TV producer, Camilla told me she had been bored. "He's not my type," she said. Too old (early forties), not attractive enough, not rich enough. She said she'd recently returned from a trip to St. Moritz with a young, titled European—that, she said, was her idea of fun. The fact that Scotty is indisputably one of the most eligible bachelors in New York meant nothing to her. She was the prize, not Scotty.

The other three women were late, so Camilla kept talking. "I'm not a bitch," she said, looking around the restaurant, "but most of the girls in New York are just idiots. Airheads. They can't even carry on a conversation. They don't know which fork to use. They don't know how to tip the maid at someone's country house."

There are a handful of women like Camilla in New York. They are all part of a sort of secret club, an urban sorority, with just a few requirements for membership: extreme beauty, youth (age range seventeen to twenty-five, or at least not admitting to being over twenty-five), brains, and the ability to sit in new restaurants for hours.

The brains part, however, appears to be relative. As one of Camilla's friends, Alexis, said, "I'm literary. I read. I'll sit down and read a whole magazine from cover to cover."

Yes, these are the beautiful girls who throw off the whole man-woman curve thing in New York, because they get more than their fair share. Of attention, invitations, gifts, and offers of clothes, money, private airplane rides, and dinners on yachts in the South of France. These are the women who accompany the bachelors with the boldface names to the best parties and charity events. The women who get asked—instead of you. They have access. New York should be their oyster. But is it?

"LET'S TALK ABOUT SCUMBAGS"

The other women showed up. Besides Camilla, who said that she was "basically single but working on" a young scion of a Park Avenue family, the women included Kitty, twenty-five, an aspiring actress who was currently living with Hubert, a still-famous-but-basically-out-of-work, fifty-five-year-old actor; Shiloh, seventeen, a model who had had a breakdown of some kind three months before and now rarely goes out; and Teesie, twenty-two, a model who had recently moved to New York and whose agency told her that she had to tell everyone she was nineteen.

The girls were all "friends," having met each other several times when they were out in the evenings, and they had even dated "some of the same scumbags," as Kitty put it.

"Let's talk about scumbags," someone said.

"Does anybody know this guy S.P.?" asked Kitty. She had long tumbledown brown hair, green eyes, a little-girl voice. "He's an old, white-haired guy with a face like a pumpkin, and he's everywhere. Well. One time, I was at Bowery Bar, and he came up to me and he said, 'You're too young to realize that you want to sleep with me and by the time you're old enough to realize it, you'll be too old for me to want to sleep with you.'"

"Men always try to buy you," said Camilla. "Once, this guy said to me, 'Please come to St. Barts with me for a weekend. We don't have to sleep together, I promise. I just want to hold you. That's all.' When he got back, he said, 'Why didn't you come with me? I told you we wouldn't sleep together.' I said, 'Don't you realize that if I go away with a man, it means I want to sleep with him?'"

"Someone at my old agency tried to sell me to some rich guy once," said Teesie. She had tiny features and a long swan neck. "This rich guy was friends with one of the bookers, and she promised him that he could 'have' me." Teesie looked outraged, then quickly motioned for the waiter. "Excuse me, but my glass has a spot on it."

Shiloh, perhaps feeling competitive, piped up: "I've had guys offer me plane tickets, I've had guys offer to fly me on their private jet. I just smile and never talk to them again."

Kitty leaned forward and said, "I had one guy offer me a breast job and an apartment. He said, 'I take care of my girls even after I break up with them.' He was a tiny, bald, Australian guy."

DASH AT THE MARK HOTEL

"Why is it that all these unattractive guys have all these ideas about what they're going to do for you?" asked Teesie.

"Most men come across as very arrogant," said Shiloh. She had skin the color of toasted almonds and long, straight black hair and huge black eyes. She was wearing a tank top and a long swirling skirt. "It's just too much for me. I finally found one guy who wasn't, but he's in India right now. I didn't feel intimidated by him. He didn't try to touch or feel me."

"There are two types of guys," said Camilla. "They're either slimeballs who are just out to get laid, or else they're in love with you instantly. It's pathetic."

"What kind of guys fall in love instantly?" Kitty wondered.

"Oh, you know," said Camilla. "Scotty. Capote Duncan. Dash Peters." Capote Duncan was the thirtysomething Southern writer who was always out with beautiful young girls. Dash Peters was a well-known Hollywood agent who was frequently in New York, also a squire of P.Y.T.'s. Both had also dated and broken the hearts of women who were in their thirties and usually pretty accomplished at something besides looking good.

"I dated Dash Peters, too," Teesie said. She touched the back of her short, dark hair. "He kept trying to get me to spend the night with him at the Mark Hotel. He sent me baskets of flowers, all white ones. He was begging me to come over and take a sauna with him. Then he wanted me to go with him to some stupid party in the Hamptons, but I wouldn't."

"I met him in the South of France," said Camilla. Sometimes Camilla spoke in a weird, fake European accent, and she was using it now.

"Did he buy you anything?" Teesie asked, trying to be casual.

"Not really," Camilla said. She motioned to the waiter. "Can you please bring me another frozen margarita?" she asked. "This one isn't cold enough." She looked back at Teesie. "Just some Chanel."

"Clothing, or accessories?"

"Clothing," Camilla said. "I already have too many Chanel bags. They bore me."

There was silence for a moment, and then Shiloh spoke up.

"I hardly ever go out anymore. I can't take it. I've become very spiritual." A thin piece of rawhide hung from her neck, twisted around a small crystal. What had finally done her in was an encounter with a famous movie actor in his early thirties who had seen her photo in a magazine and tracked down her agency. They passed on his number, and because she had just seen him in a movie and thought he was cute, she called him. He invited her to spend two weeks with him at his house in Los Angeles. Then he came to New York, and he started to get weird. He refused to go out, except to strip clubs, where he tried to get girls to do special things to him for free, "because he was famous," Shiloh said.

Kitty put her elbows on the table. "A couple of years ago, I said, 'I've been screwed over too many times.' So I decided to take a guy's virginity and then leave him. I was bad, but on the other hand, he was twenty-one, which is probably too old to be a virgin, so he deserved it. I was as sweet as could be, and then I never talked to him again. It doesn't matter how pretty you are. If you can create who the guy wants you to be, you can get him."

"If a guy says to me, 'I like fishnets and red lipstick,' I see it as accessorizing," said Teesie.

"If Hubert was a girl, he'd be the trashiest girl you've ever seen," said Kitty. "I said, 'Yes, I'll wear short skirts, but I'm going to wear underwear underneath.' One time, I had to totally get him back. He kept harassing me and harassing me to sleep with him and another woman. Finally, I have this friend who's gay? George? And we kiss sometimes, but it's like kids? So I said, 'Honey, George is coming over and he's going to spend the night.' Hubert was like, 'Where is he going to sleep?' I said, 'Oh, I thought he'd sleep in the bed with us. And you're going to play receiver.' He totally freaked out. I said, 'Honey, if you really love me, you'll do this for me because it's what I want.' Well," she said, ordering another margarita. "It had to be done. Now we're on a level that's equal."

"HELLO, KITTY"

"Older guys are gross," said Camilla. "I won't go out with them anymore. A couple of years ago, I realized, why do I need to go out with these ugly, rich old men, when I can go out with gorgeous, rich young guys? Plus, these old guys don't really understand you. No matter how much they think they do. They're another generation."

"I don't think older guys are so bad," Kitty said. "Of course, when Hubert first called me up and said he wanted to go out with me, I was like, 'How old are you and how much hair do you have left on your head?' He really had to woo me. The first time he came to pick me up, I walked out with dirty hair and no makeup. It was like, If you want me so much, get a look at the real me. And after that, the first time I spent the night with him, the next morning I woke up, and he had a bouquet of my favorite flowers in every room. He found out who my favorite author was, and he bought all the books. On the mirror, he wrote in shaving cream, 'Hello, Kitty.'"

The women squealed. "That is so adorable," Teesie said. "I love men."

"I love men too, but sometimes I need a break from them," Shiloh said.

"Hubert loves it when I mess up," said Kitty. "He loves it when I buy too many clothes, and I can't pay the bill. He loves to step in and take care of everything.

"Men are needy, and we're the goddesses that give to them," Kitty said triumphantly. She was well into her second margarita. "On the other hand, men are . . . bigger. Larger. They're comfort."

"They give you something that women can't," Shiloh said, nodding. "A man should provide for his girlfriend."

"Hubert makes me feel really safe. He's allowing me to have the childhood I never had," said Kitty. "I don't buy this whole feminist idea. Men have a need to be dominant—let them. Embrace your femininity."

"I think men can be complicated, but I always know there's another one out there if this one doesn't work out," said Teesie. "Men are not high maintenance."

"It's other women who are really the problem," said Camilla.

"At the risk of sounding obnoxious, being beautiful is such a power, you can get whatever you want," said Kitty. "And other women know that and don't like you, especially older women. They think you're invading their territory."

"For a lot of women, when they reach thirty, they start to realize their age," said Camilla. "Men have given women this stigma. Obviously, a woman who looks like Christie Brinkley is not going to have a problem."

"But they get mean," said Kitty. "They make comments. Women just assume that I'm an idiot. That I don't know anything. That I'm stupid. That I'm with Hubert for his money. You get spiteful and wear an even shorter skirt and more makeup."

"Nobody bothers to ask. They just assume," said Teesie.

"Women are so envious in general," said Shiloh. "It doesn't have anything to do with their age. It's disgusting. They see an attractive girl, and they give attitude. It's so sad and shocking. It's so telling of where women are in their lives. They're so insecure and unhappy about where they are, they can't stand it if it seems like another woman has it better."

"That's why most of my friends are men." The three other women looked around the table and nodded.

What about sex? someone asked.

"I tell every guy they have the biggest thing I've ever seen," said Kitty. The women laughed nervously. Kitty slurped up the last bit of her margarita through a straw. "It's survival," she said.

14

Portrait of a Bulgy Underwear Model: The Bone Pops Out of His Giant Billboard

A door opens at the top of the stairs and the Bone, an underwear model and budding actor, stands silhouetted in the doorway of his apartment. One arm is up and he's leaning against the doorframe and his dark brown hair is falling in his face and he's laughing as he watches you trudge breathless up the stairs.

"You're always on the go," he says, like all he wants to do is lie around in bed all day. You remember what his friend, screenwriter Stanford Blatch, keeps telling you: "The Bone looks like he travels with his own lighting director." And then it's too much: You have to look away.

"The Bone is the human equivalent of a sable coat," Stanford says. Stanford has been bugging you a lot about the Bone lately. The phone rings and you pick it up and it's Stanford. "Who's sexier? The Bone or Keanu Reeves?" You sigh. And even though you sort of really don't know who the Bone is and don't really care, you say, "The Bone."

Maybe it's partly out of guilt. You know that you should know who he is: He's that guy who was splashed—muscled, nearly naked—on that giant billboard in Times Square, and he was all over the buses. But you never go to Times Square and you don't pay attention to buses, except when they're about to hit you.

But Stanford keeps working on you. "The Bone and I were walking by his billboard the other day," he says, "and the Bone wanted to get a piece of it to put in his apartment, like maybe his nose. But I told him he should take the bulge in his pants. That way, when women ask him how big he is, he can say fourteen feet.

"The Bone did the cutest thing today," Stanford says. "He tried to take me out to dinner. He said, 'Stanford, you've done so much for me, I want to do something for you.' I said, 'Don't be silly,' but you know, he is the only person who's ever offered to take me out to dinner in my whole life. Can you believe anyone that beautiful is that nice?"

You agree to meet the Bone.

"YOU'RE GOING TO BE A STAR"

The first time you meet the Bone, at Bowery Bar with Stanford at his side, you want to hate him. He's twenty-two. A model. Et cetera. You pretty much sense that he wants to hate you, too. Is he going to be really stupid? Besides, you don't think sex symbols are ever really sexy in person. The last one you met reminded you of a worm. Literally.

But not this one. He's not exactly what he appears to be.

"I have different personalities with different people," he says. Then you lose him in the crowd.

About two months later, you're at that model's birthday party at Barocco, and you run into the Bone. He's standing across the room, leaning against the bar, and he's smiling at you. He waves. You go over. He keeps hugging you, and photographers keep taking your picture. Then, you somehow end up sitting across the table from him. You and your friend are having this huge, never-ending, heated argument.

The Bone keeps leaning over and asking you if you're okay. And you say yes, thinking he doesn't understand that you and your friend always talk to each other that way.

Stanford, who knows everyone in Hollywood, sends the Bone out to L.A. to go on auditions for small parts in movies. He leaves Stanford a message. "Everyone's talking about you," he says. "You are so great. You're going to be a star. Have I told you that enough times yet? You're a star, you're a star, you're a star."

Stanford is laughing. "He's imitating me," he says.

You and the Bone get drunk at Bowery Bar.

AN EASY "A"

The Bone lives in a tiny studio that has white everything: white curtains, white sheets, white comforter, white chaise. When you're in the bathroom, you look to see if he uses special cosmetics. He doesn't.

The Bone grew up in Des Moines, Iowa. His father was a teacher. His mother was the school nurse. In high school, the Bone didn't hang out with the cool kids. He used to make straight A's and tutor younger children after school. They all looked up to him.

The Bone never thought about becoming a model, but when he was in eighth grade, he was voted best-looking guy. He secretly wanted to do something exciting. Like being a detective. But he went to the University of Iowa and studied literature for two years. It was what his father wanted. One of his teachers was young and good-looking, and when he called the Bone in for a meeting, he sat next to him and put his hand on the Bone's leg. He slid his hand up to the bulge in the Bone's pants. "This could be an easy A for you," he said. The Bone never went back to his class. Three months later, he dropped out of college.

Recently, someone's been calling the Bone's apartment and leaving messages that are only music. At first, he listened to the songs, because he kept thinking the music was going to stop and one of his friends would start talking. Now, he listens to the songs to see if there's a clue. "I think it's a man," he says.

AN IOWA BOYHOOD

You're lying on the bed with the Bone, like you're both twelve (lying on your stomach and hanging your legs over the side), and you say, "Tell me a story." He says, "The story I'm thinking about the most lately is my ex, ex-girlfriend."

It was the summer of 1986 and the Bone was fourteen. It was one of those summer days in Iowa when the sky is clear and the corn in the fields is so green. And the whole summer, when you drive around in the car with your friends, you see the corn grow.

The Bone and his family went to the state fair. The Bone was walking through the livestock exhibit with his friend when he saw her. She was brushing a baby heifer, and he grabbed his friend's arm and he said, "That's going to be my wife!"

He didn't see her again for a whole year. Then, one evening, he was at one of those youth dances that they have in small towns to keep the teens out of trouble, and she was there. He fooled around with her on Christmas Eve. "Then I got totally dumped," he says. "It really hurt in a weird way."

A year and a half later, when she decided she wanted him, he didn't give in. "Even though I wanted to be with her so bad," he says. "Then one day I gave in."

The Bone went out with her on and off for a few years. She's a computer programmer in Iowa City. But they still talk. Maybe he'll marry her someday? He grins, and when he does, his nose wrinkles at the top. "I might," he says. "I always think it's such a beautiful story in my head. It blows my mind away."

"The Bone is always saying that he could move back to Iowa and have kids and be a cop," Stanford says.

"It's adorable, as long as he doesn't really do it," you say, then feel cynical for having said it.

"I KNOW I'M NEUROTIC"

You and the Bone are hungry, so you go to Bagels "R" Us at six in the evening on a Sunday. Two female cops sit in the corner smoking. People are wearing dirty sweat clothes. The Bone eats half of your ham and cheese sandwich. "I could eat four of these sandwiches," he says, "but I won't. If I eat a hamburger, I feel so guilty afterward."

The Bone cares about the way he looks. "I change my clothes about five times a day," he says. "Who doesn't look in the mirror about a hundred times before they go out? I go back and forth between the two mirrors in my apartment like I'm going to look different in each one. It's like, yeah, I look good in this mirror, let me see if I look as good in the other. Doesn't everyone do that?"

"Sometimes I get so distracted," the Bone says. "My thoughts get so scattered in my head. It's jumbled and it doesn't make sense."

"What's distracting you now?" you ask.

"Your nose."

"Thanks a lot. I hate my nose."

"I hate my nose, too," he says. "It's too big. But I think it depends on my hair. The other day Stanford said, 'I like your hair like that. It's full. It makes your nose look smaller.'" You both crack up.

Back on the street, the Bone nudges you. "They spelled puppies wrong," he says. You look. A man in overalls is standing next to a giant gray mastiff and holding a cardboard sign that says, PUPPYS FOR SALE.

"Huh?" the man says. There's a dirty red and white truck parked behind him.

"Puppies. You spelled it wrong," the Bone says.

The man looks at the sign and grins.

"Hey, they're selling the same puppies up the street for two hundred dollars instead of two thousand," the Bone says, and the man laughs.

Later, you're sitting on the edge of the bed with your head in your hands staring at the Bone, who's lying on the bed with one hand in the waistband of his jeans.

"One minute, I could be walking down the street totally cool, and the next minute I'm depressed for no reason," he says. "I know I'm neurotic. I see it. I feel it. I'm self-analytical, self-critical, self-conscious. I'm very aware of everything I say."

Then the Bone says, "Before I say something, I say it in my head first, so it doesn't come out wrong."

"Doesn't that kind of seem like a waste of time?" you ask.

"It only takes a second."

He pauses. "If I'm out, and a stranger comes up to me and asks me if I'm a model, I say, 'No, I'm a student.'"

"And?"

The Bone laughs. "They lose interest," he says, looking at you like he can't believe you didn't know that.

Stanford calls you up. "The Bone left me the cutest message," he says. And he plays it. "Stannie, did you die? Are you dead? You must be dead because you're not answering your phone. [Laughing.] Call me later."

"IVANA TRUMP'S BUTLER?"

You like hanging out with the Bone in his apartment. It reminds you of when you were sixteen, in your own small town in Connecticut, and you used to hang out with this guy who was really beautiful and you'd smoke pot and your parents would think you were off riding your horse. They'd never know the truth.

You look out his window at the sunlight on the backs of tatty little brownstones. "I've wanted to have kids ever since I was a kid," the Bone says. "It's my dream."

But that was before. Before all this stuff happened to the Bone. Before now.

A couple of weeks ago, the Bone got offered a second lead in an ensemble movie starring all the cool young Hollywood actors. He went to a party and accidentally ended up going home with one of the other actors' girlfriends, a new supermodel. The actor threatened to kill the Bone and the supermodel, and she and the Bone temporarily fled the city. Only Stanford knows where they are. Stanford calls and says he's been on the phone constantly. *Hard Copy* offered the Bone money to appear, and Stanford said to them, "Who do you think he is—Ivana Trump's butler?"

The Bone says, "I just don't believe the bullshit. It's still me. I haven't changed. People are always telling me, Don't ever change. What am I going to change into? An egomaniac? A prick? An asshole? I know myself really well. What do I want to change into?"

"Why are you laughing?" he asks.

"I'm not laughing," you say. "I'm crying."

Stanford says, "Have you ever noticed how the Bone has no scent whatsoever?"

15

He Loves His Little Mouse, but He Won't Take Her Home to Mom

This is a story about a dirty little secret in the dating world. Almost everybody's been there—on one side or the other.

Two men were sitting at the Princeton Club having drinks. It was late afternoon. Both men were in their early thirties and had once been pretty-boy preppies. They were now losing their looks, and both had an extra twelve pounds around their middles that they couldn't lose. They'd gone to college together and had moved to New York after graduation. They were good friends; they had the kind of friendship that tends to be unusual for men. They could actually talk about things. Like diets that didn't work. And women.

Walden had just been made partner in a corporate law firm and had recently gotten engaged to a dermatologist. Stephen had been in a relationship for three years. He was a producer on a network magazine show.

Walden's fiancée was out of town at a collagen convention. On his own, Walden always got lonely. It reminded him of a time when he had really been lonely, for months on end that seemed to drag into years. And it always brought him around to the same memory, of the woman who had made him feel better, and of what he'd done to her.

Walden met her at a party filled with very pretty people. This being Manhattan, she was nicely dressed in a short black dress that showed off breasts that were on the large side. But she had a modest face. Beautiful long black hair, though. Ringlets. "They always have one great feature," Walden said, and took a sip of his martini.

There was something about this girl, Libby. She was sitting on a couch by herself, and she didn't seem uncomfortable. Another girl came by, a pretty girl, and she leaned down and whispered something in Libby's ear, and Libby laughed. But she didn't get up. Walden was standing by the side of the couch, drinking beer out of the bottle. He was thinking about which pretty girl to approach, looking for openings. Libby caught his eye and smiled. She looked friendly. He sat down, figuring it was a momentary oasis.

He kept thinking that he was going to get up and approach one of the pretty girls, but he didn't. Libby had gone to Columbia undergrad, Harvard grad school. She talked to him about law. She told him about her childhood, growing up with four sisters in North Carolina. She was twenty-four and had a grant to make a documentary. She leaned forward and removed a hair from his sweater. "Mine," she said, and laughed. They talked for a long time. He finished a second beer.

"Do you want to come over to my place?" she asked.

He did. He figured he knew what was going to happen. They'd have sex for one night, he'd go home the next day and forget about it. Like most men in New York, he made up his mind about a woman right away. Put her in a category—one-night stand, potential girlfriend, hot two-week fling. Back then, he was sleeping with plenty of women, and eventually there would be tearful scenes in his lobby and sometimes worse.

Libby was definitely a one-night stand. She wasn't pretty enough to date, to be seen in public with.

"But what does that mean, really?" Stephen interrupted.

"I just thought she was uglier than me," Walden said.

When they got to Libby's apartment—a basic two-bedroom in a high-rise on Third Avenue that she shared with her cousin—she opened the refrigerator and took out a beer. When she bent over in the refrigerator light, he saw that she was a little on the heavy side. She turned around and unscrewed the cap and handed the bottle to him. "I just want you to know," she said. "I really want to have sex with you."

A pretty girl wouldn't have said that, he thought, as he put down his beer and began undressing her. He bit her neck and pulled down the top of her bra without unhooking it. He peeled off her pantyhose. She wasn't wearing underwear. They went into the bedroom.

"I found myself very uninhibited," Walden said. "Because she wasn't pretty. The stakes were lower, the emotion higher. There wasn't any pressure because I knew I couldn't date her." He fell asleep with his arms around her.

"The next morning," Walden said, "I woke up and I felt at ease. Very relaxed. I'd been feeling tormented for some time, and, with Libby, I suddenly felt peaceful. It was the first honest emotional connection I'd had in a while. So I immediately panicked and had to leave."

He walked home with his hands in his pockets. It was winter and he'd left his gloves at her place.

"It's always winter when these things happen," Stephen said.

"ACTUAL FRIENDS"

Walden didn't see her again for a few months. He went back to his torment. If she was better-looking, he would have gone out with her. Instead, he waited two months, then he called her for lunch. He'd been fantasizing about her. They had lunch, and then they blew off the afternoon and went back to her place and had sex. They began seeing each other a couple of times a week. They lived in the same neighborhood; they'd go to local places for dinner or she'd cook. "I found it incredibly easy to talk about my emotions," Walden said. "I could cry in front of her. I told her my deepest sexual fantasies and we'd act them out. We talked about having a threesome with one of her friends.

"She'd tell me her fantasies, which were tremendously elaborate," Walden continued. "She asked me to spank her. She had secrets, but she was incredibly practical. I've always wondered if it was because she wasn't datable that she'd constructed this complicated inner life. You know, if you're not in the beauty Olympics, you can become a very interesting person."

In the meantime, Libby was being pursued by, in Walden's words, "some shlumpy guy." Walden didn't feel threatened.

He met all her friends but wouldn't introduce her to his. He never spent a whole weekend with her—or even a whole day. They never went to a party together. "I didn't want her to get the wrong idea," he said.

But she never protested, never made demands. One time she asked him if the reason he kept her hidden was because she wasn't pretty enough. "I lied and said no," Walden said. "You know, if I closed my eyes, there was no way she didn't satisfy me in every way."

Walden ordered another drink. "She used to make me wonder if I felt ugly inside, and that was the bond."

"Well, every man secretly hates pretty girls because they're the ones who rejected him in high school," Stephen said. He had a similar story.

Ellen's grandfather was famous in TV. A real big deal. Stephen met her at a work party. They'd both gone outside on the balcony to smoke cigarettes and started talking. She was funny. A real firecracker, a wiseacre. She was dating somebody else. After that, she and Stephen would run into each other at work events.

"We became actual friends," said Stephen, "which for me is rare with women. I had no sexual designs on her. I could go out with her and shoot the shit like a guy. She could talk about movies, Letterman, she knew TV—and most women don't understand TV. If you try to talk about TV with a pretty girl, her eyes glaze over."

They went to the movies, but "just as friends." She might have been secretly angling for him; but if she was, Stephen didn't notice. They'd talk about their relationships. Their dissatisfactions. Stephen was seeing someone who had gone to Europe for three months, and he was writing her forced, unenthusiastic letters.

One afternoon, they were having lunch, when Ellen began describing a recent sexual encounter with her boyfriend. She had given him a hand job using Vaseline. Stephen suddenly popped a woody. "I began to see her as a sexual being," he said. "The thing about these girls who aren't beauties—they have to put sex on the table. They can't nuance it."

Ellen broke up with her boyfriend, and Stephen began dating lots of women. He would tell Ellen about these women. One night they were at a restaurant, having dinner, and Ellen leaned over and gave him a tongue kiss in his ear that got him thumping his foot.

They went to her place and had sex. "It was great," Stephen said. "I performed, on an objective basis, better than I had with other women. I was going back for seconds and thirds. I was giving her the forty-five-minute fuck." The "relationship" progressed from there. They would watch TV in bed and then have sex with the TV on. "A pretty woman would never let you have the TV on during sex," Stephen said. "But it's relaxing somehow, with the TV on. You're not the focus. Women like Ellen allow you to be yourself."

Stephen admitted that from Ellen's point of view, their relationship probably wasn't so great. "During the six months we went out, well, we had probably gone to more movies back when we were friends. Our dates became the worst kind of dates—takeout food and videos. I felt tremendously guilty. I felt shallow. She wasn't quite up to snuff in the looks department, and I felt shallow for thinking of her looks. She was a great girl."

THEN SHE BROKE

Ellen started in with the pressure. "'When are you going to meet my grandfather,' she kept asking me. 'He really wants to meet you.'"

"I wanted to meet her grandfather," Stephen said. "He was a huge deal. But I couldn't. When you meet someone's grandparents, it means the relationship is real."

To solve his problem, Stephen began pimping for Ellen, trying to fix her up with guys. They would talk about guys she could date. One night, Ellen went to a party where she was supposed to meet one of Stephen's friends. But the guy wasn't interested in her and she got upset. She went to Stephen's place and they had sex.

A couple of weeks later, Stephen met a girl, a babe, late one night at a party in a grungy loft in TriBeCa. He introduced her to his parents almost immediately, even though he had none of the kinds of conversations with her that he had with Ellen. He continued to sleep with both girls, taking what he had learned from sex with Ellen and applying it to the new girl. Ellen wanted to hear all about it. What they did. What the new girl was like in bed, what she felt like, what they talked about.

Then she broke. She went to Stephen's apartment on a Sunday afternoon. They had a screaming fight. She was punching him, "literally raining down punches on me," Stephen said. She left but called two weeks later.

"We made up on the phone," Stephen said, "and I went to her house for the usual. But when we got to the crucial moment, she kicked me out of bed. I didn't get mad at her.

I was too angry with myself for that, but I respected her, too. I thought, Good for you."

Walden put a knee up against the bar. "About six months after I stopped seeing Libby, she got engaged. She called me and said she was getting married."

"I was in love with Ellen but I never told her," Stephen said.

"I was in love, too," Walden said. "In love in an utterly mundane way."

16

Clueless in Manhattan

There are worse things than being thirty-five, single, and female in New York. Like: Being twenty-five, single, and female in New York.

It's a rite of passage few women would want to repeat. It's about sleeping with the wrong men, wearing the wrong clothes, having the wrong roommate, saying the wrong thing, being ignored, getting fired, not being taken seriously, and generally being treated like shit. But it's necessary. So if you've ever wondered how thirty-five-year-old, single, New York women get to be, well, thirty-five-year-old, single, New York women, read on.

A couple of weeks ago, Carrie ran into Cici, a twenty-five-year-old assistant to a flower designer, at the Louis Vuitton party. Carrie was trying to say hello to five people at once when Cici materialized out of the semidarkness. "Hiiiiii," she said, and when Carrie glanced over at her, she said, "Hiiiii," again. Then she just stared.

Carrie had to turn away from a book editor she was talking to. "What, Cici?" she asked. *"What is it?"*

"I don't know. How are you?"

"I'm fine. Fabulous," Carrie said.

"What have you been up to?"

"The usual." The book editor was about to talk to someone else. "Cici, I . . ."

"I haven't seen you for so long," Cici said. "I miss you. You know I'm your biggest fan. Other people say you're a bitch, but I say, 'No, she's one of my best friends and she's not like that.' I defend you."

"Thanks."

Cici just stood there, staring. "How are *you?*" Carrie asked.

"Great," Cici said. "Every night I get all dressed up and I go out and no one pays attention to me and I go home and cry."

"Oh, Cici," Carrie said. Then: "Don't worry about it. It's just a phase. Now listen, I have to . . ."

"I know," Cici said. "You don't have time for me. It's okay. I'll talk to you later." And she walked away.

Cici York and her best friend, Carolyne Everhardt, are two twenty-five year olds who, like most now thirty-five year olds, came to New York to have careers.

Carolyne Everhardt is a nightlife writer for a downtown publication. Came here from Texas three years ago. She's one of those girls with a beautiful face, who is just a bit overweight but not concerned about it—at least not to the point that she'd ever let you think she was.

Cici is the opposite of Carolyne—blond, bone-thin, with one of those oddly elegant faces that most people don't notice because she isn't convinced that she is beautiful. Cici works as an assistant to Yorgi, the acclaimed yet reclusive flower designer.

Cici came to New York a year and a half ago from Philadelphia. "Back then, I was like a little Mary Tyler Moore," she says. "I actually had white gloves stashed in my purse. For the first six months, I didn't even go out. I was too scared about keeping my job."

And now? "We're not nice girls. Nice is not a word you would apply to us," Cici says, in an East Coast drawl that manages to be sexy and apathetic.

"We mortify people all the time," Carolyne says.

"Carolyne is known for her *temper tantrums,*" Cici says.

"And Cici doesn't talk to people. She just gives them dirty looks."

ARABIAN NIGHTS

Carolyne and Cici are best friends through the usual conduit of bonding female friendship in New York: Over some jerky guy.

Before she met Cici, Carolyne met Sam, forty-two, an investment banker. Carolyne kept running into him every time she went out. Sam had a girlfriend—a Swiss girl who was trying to get into broadcasting. One night, Sam and Carolyne saw each other at Spy and they were drunk, and they started making out. They ran into each other another night and went back to Sam's place and had sex. This happened a couple more times. Then his girlfriend got deported.

Nevertheless, the "relationship" continued along the same lines. Every time Carolyne and Sam ran into each other, they would have sex. One night, she saw him at System and gave him a hand job in the corner. Then they went outside and had sex behind a Dumpster in an alleyway. Afterward, Sam zipped up his pants, kissed her on the cheek, and said, "Well, thanks a lot. I'll see you later." Carolyne started throwing trash at him. "I'm not through with you, Samuel," she said.

A couple of weeks later, Cici was at Casa La Femme, when she saw two guys she knew. A third guy was with them. He was dark and he was wearing a thin, white, button-down shirt and khakis; Cici could tell that he had a great body. He seemed shy, and Cici began flirting with him. She'd just gotten her hair cut, and she kept brushing her bangs out of her eyes and looking up at him while sipping a glass of champagne. They were all going to some girl's birthday party at a loft in SoHo; they asked Cici to go with them. They walked. Cici kept giggling and bumping into the guy, and at one point he put his arm around her. "How old are you?" he asked.

"Twenty-four."

"Perfect age," he said.

"Perfect? For what?" Cici asked.

"Me," he said.

"How old are you?" Cici asked.

"Thirty-six," he said. Lying.

The party was crowded. Beer in a keg, vodka and gin in plastic glasses. Cici had just turned away from the bar and was about to take a sip of beer when she saw an apparition barreling toward her from the other side of the loft. A large girl with long dark hair, wearing red lipstick and, rather inexplicably, a long "dress" (If you can call it that, Cici thought) that appeared to be made of flowered chiffon scarves. Arabian Nights.

The guy turned just as she was about to run into them. "Carolyne!" he said. "Love your dress."

"Thanks, Sam," Carolyne said.

"Is that that new designer you were telling me about?" Sam asked. "The one who was going to make you a bunch of dresses for free if you wrote about him?" He smirked.

"Would you shut up?" Carolyne screamed. She turned to Cici. "Who are you, and what are you doing at my birthday party?"

"He invited me," Cici said.

"So you just accept invitations from other girls' boyfriends, huh?"

"Carolyne. I am not your boyfriend," Sam said.

"Oh yeah. You've just slept with me about twenty times. What about last time. That hand job at System?"

"You gave someone a hand job at a club?" Cici asked.

"Carolyne. I have a girlfriend," Sam said.

"She got deported. And now you can't keep your greedy little hands off me."

"She's back," Sam said. "She's living in my apartment."

"You have a girlfriend?" Cici asked.

"You mortify me," Carolyne said to Sam. "Get out and take your cheap little slut with you."

"You have a girlfriend?" Cici asked again. She kept repeating it, all the way down the stairs until they were out on the street.

Two weeks later, Carolyne ran into Cici in the bathroom at a club.

"I just wanted to tell you that I saw Sam," Carolyne said, applying red lipstick. "He got down on his hands and knees and begged me to go back to him. He said I was beyond."

"Beyond what?" Cici said, pretending to check her mascara in the mirror.

"Did you fool around with him?" Carolyne asked. She snapped the top back on her lipstick.

"No," Cici said. "I don't fool around with anybody."

Sure enough, Carolyne and Cici became best friends.

"I HATE MIAMI"

Carrie met Cici around this time last year at Bowery Bar. Carrie was sitting at one of the booths, it was kind of late and she was kind of fucked up, and this girl bounced over and said stuff like, "You're my idol" and "You're so beautiful" and "Where did you get your shoes I love them." Carrie was flattered. "I want to be your best friend," Cici said, in a voice that rubbed up against her like a cat. "Can I be your best friend? Please?"

"Now listen, er . . ."

"Cici."

"Cici," Carrie said, a little sternly. "It just doesn't work that way."

"Why not?"

"Because I've been in New York for fifteen years. Fifteen years and . . ."

"Oh," Cici said, slumping. "But can I call you? I'm going to call you." And then she bounced over to another table, sat down, turned around, and waved.

A couple of weeks later, Cici called Carrie. "You've got to come to Miami with us."

"I hate Miami. I will never step foot in Miami," Carrie said. "If you ever call me again and mention Miami, I will hang up."

"You are just so funny," Cici said.

In Miami, Cici and Carolyne stayed with some rich-guy friends of Carolyne's from the University of Texas. On Friday night, they all went out and got drunk, and Cici made out with one of the Texas guys, Dexter. But she got annoyed at him the following night when he followed her around, putting his arm around her, trying to kiss her—like they were a couple or something. "Let's go upstairs and fool around," he kept whispering in her ear. Cici didn't want to, so she sort of started ignoring him, and Dexter stormed out of the house. He came back a couple of hours later with a girl. "Hi y'all," he said, giving Cici a wave as he passed by the living room on his way upstairs with the girl. The girl gave him a blow job. Then they came downstairs, and Dexter made a great show of writing down her phone number.

Cici ran out of the house screaming and crying just as Carolyne was spinning up the driveway in a rental car. She was also screaming and crying. She'd run into Sam, who just happened to be in Miami as well, and he had wanted her to have a ménage à trois with some blond, stripper bimbo, and when Carolyne said, "Fuck off," he pushed her down on the sand at South Beach and said, "The only reason I ever went anyplace with you was because we always get our pictures taken at parties."

PAGE SIX!

Two weeks later, Carolyne ended up in the *Post*'s "Page Six" gossip column. She went to some party at the Tunnel, and when the doorman wouldn't let her in, she started screaming at him; he tried to escort her to a cab, she punched him, he wrestled her to the ground, and the next day she made the publisher of the downtown publication she worked for call up the Tunnel and try to get the guy fired, and then she called up "Page Six." When the item came out, she bought twenty copies of the paper.

Then Cici got kicked out of the apartment she was sharing with a lawyer from Philadelphia—the older sister of one of her high school friends. The woman said, "Cici, you've changed. I'm really worried about you. You're not a nice person anymore and I don't know what to do." Cici yelled at her that she was just jealous, then she moved to Carolyne's couch.

Around that time, an unfortunate item came out about Carrie in one of the gossip columns. She was trying to ignore it when Cici called up all excited.

"Omigod, you're famous," she said. "You're in the papers. Have you read it?" Then she began reading it, and it was awful, so Carrie started screaming at her. "Let me explain something. If you want to survive in this town, never, ever call anybody up and read something terrible about them from the papers. You pretend you never saw it, okay? And if they ask you if you did, you lie and say, 'No, I don't read trash like that.' Even though you do. Get it? Jesus, Cici," she said, "whose side are you on here?" Cici started crying, and Carrie hung up the phone and felt guilty afterward.

MR. RESIDUE

"I'm going to introduce you to a guy, and I know you're going to fall in love with him, but don't," Carolyne said to Cici. So she did.

Ben was forty, a sometime restaurateur and party promoter who'd already been married twice (in fact, he was still married, but his wife had gone back to Florida) and been in and out of rehab a dozen times. Everyone in New York knew about him, and when his name came up, people would roll their eyes and change the subject. After all his drinking and coke snorting, he still possessed a residue of what he was before—charming, amusing, handsome—and Cici fell in love with the residue. They spent two great weekends together, even though they never actually had sex. Then they went to a party, he disappeared, and Cici found him rubbing up against a sixteen-year-old model who had just come to town. "You're disgusting!" she screamed.

"Oh, *come on,*" he said. "You've got to let me live out my fantasies. I have a fantasy of being with a sixteen year old." He grinned, and you could see that his teeth needed to be rebonded.

The next morning, Cici turned up uninvited at his apartment. His three-year-old daughter was visiting. "I brought you a present," she said, acting like nothing had happened. The present was a baby bunny. She put it on the couch, and it peed several times.

Meanwhile, Carolyne sort of moved in with Sam. She kept her apartment but spent every night at his and always left something—shoes, perfume, earrings, dry-cleaned blouses, six or seven different kinds of face cream—behind. This went on for three months. The night before Valentine's Day, he exploded. "I want you out," he said. "Out!" He was screaming and breathing heavily.

"I don't get it," Carolyne said.

"There's nothing *to* get," Sam said. "I just want you, and your stuff, out of here now!" Sam cranked open a window and began throwing her things out.

Carolyne said, "I'll fix your wagon, buster," and she smacked him hard across the back of his head.

He turned around. "You hit me," he said.

"Sam . . . ," she said.

"I can't believe . . . you hit me." He began backing across the floor. "Don't come near me," he said. He cautiously reached down and picked up his cat.

"Sam," Carolyne said, walking toward him.

"Stay back," he said. He grabbed the cat under its armpits so its legs were sticking straight out at Carolyne; he held it up like a weapon. "I said, get back."

"Sam. Sam." Carolyne shook her head. "This is so pity-ful."

"Not to me," Sam said. He hurried into the bedroom, cradling the cat in his arms. "She's a witch, isn't she, Puffy?" he asked the cat. "A real witch."

Carolyne took a few steps toward the bed. "I didn't mean . . ."

"You hit me," Sam said in a weird, little-boy voice. "Don't ever hit me. Don't hit Sam no more."

"Okay . . . ," Carolyne said cautiously.

The cat struggled out of Sam's arms. It ran across the floor. "Here kitty kitty," Carolyne said. "C'mere kitty. Want some milk?" She heard the TV click on.

"HE WAS SO MORTIFIED"

Carrie was always promising Cici and Carolyne that she'd have dinner with them, so one day, she finally did. On a Sunday night. Her only free night. Carolyne and Cici were sitting back on the banquette, their legs crossed, stirring their drinks, and looking very smart. Carolyne was talking on a cellular phone. "I have to go out every night for my job," Cici said, sounding bored. "I'm just so *tired* all the time."

Carolyne flipped her cellular phone closed and looked at Carrie. "We've got to go to this party tonight. Downtown. Lots of models. You should come," she said, in a tone that suggested she definitely should not.

"Well, how *is* everything?" Carrie said. "You know, like Sam and . . ."

"Everything is fine," Carolyne said.

Cici lit a cigarette and looked off in another direction. "Sam went around telling everyone that he and Carolyne had never slept together, even though tons of people had seen them making out, so we mortified him."

"We found out he started seeing this girl who has diseases, so I called him up and I said, 'Sam, please, as a friend, promise me you won't sleep with her,'" Carolyne said.

"Then we saw the two of them at this brunch place."

"We were dressed to the nines. They were wearing sweatpants. We went up to them and they asked us for a cigarette and we said, 'A cigarette? Oh please. Get one from the waiter.'"

"We sat right next to them. *Intentionally*. They kept trying to talk to us, and Carolyne kept making calls on her cellular phone. Then I said, 'Sam, how's that girl I saw you with last week?'"

"He was so mortified. We sent him notes saying, 'Herpes simplex 19.'"

"Is there a herpes simplex 19?" Carrie asked.

"No," Cici said. "Don't you *get* it?"

"Right," Carrie said. She didn't say anything for a minute while she took a long time to light a cigarette, then she said, "What is *wrong* with you?"

"Nothing," Cici said. "The only thing I care about is my career. Like you. You're my *idol*."

Then the two girls looked at their watches and each other.

"Do you mind," Cici said. "We have to go to this party."

17

City in Heat! Sexual
Panic Seizes Mr. Big

Manhattan's Own Brand
of Summertime Steaminess Gives
Way to Sidewalk Fantasies,
Drunken Jigs, Bedroom Crackups,
and Air-Conditioned Nightmares

New York is a completely different city in August. Like living in some South American country with a corrupt and drunk dictator, skyrocketing inflation, drug cartels, dust-covered roads, clogged plumbing—where nothing will ever get better, the rains will never come.

The psyche of most New Yorkers cracks under the heat. Bad thoughts and bad feelings bubble to the surface. They lead to bad behavior, the kind New Yorkers specialize in. It's secretive. It's nasty. Relationships break up. People who shouldn't be together get together.

The city's in heat. Days of ninety-five-plus–degree weather are strung together one after the other. Everyone is cranky.

In the heat, you can't trust anyone, especially yourself.

Carrie is lying in Mr. Big's bed at eight A.M. She believes she is not going to be okay. In fact, she is pretty damn sure that she is not going to be okay. She's crying hysterically into the pillow.

"Carrie. Calm down. Calm down," Mr. Big orders. She rolls over, and her face is a grotesque, blotchy mask.

"You're going to be okay. I have to go to work now. Right now. You're keeping me from work."

"Can you help me?" Carrie asks.

"No," he says, sliding his gold cufflinks through the holes of starched cuffs. "You have to help yourself. Figure it out."

Carrie puts her head under the covers, still crying. "Call me in a couple of hours," he says, then walks out of the room. "Goodbye."

Two minutes later, he comes back. "I forgot my cigar case," he says, watching her as he crosses the room. She's quiet now.

"Goodbye," he says. "Goodbye. Goodbye."

It's the tenth day in a row of suffocating heat and humidity.

MR. BIG'S HEAT RITUAL

Carrie has been spending too much time with Mr. Big. He has air conditioning. She does, too, but hers doesn't work. They develop a little ritual. A heat ritual. Every evening at eleven, if they haven't been out together, Mr. Big calls.

"How's your apartment?" he asks.

"Hot," she says.

"What are you doing then?"

"Sweating."

"Do you want to come over and sleep here?" he asks, almost a little shyly.

"Sure, why not," she says. She yawns.

Then she races around her apartment, flies out the door (past the night doorman, who always gives her dirty looks), and jumps into a cab.

"Oh, hiiii," Mr. Big says when he opens the door, naked. He says it half-sleepy, as if he's surprised to see her.

They get into bed. Letterman or Leno. Mr. Big has one pair of glasses. They take turns wearing them.

"Have you ever thought about getting a new air conditioner?" Mr. Big asks.

"Yes," Carrie says.

"You can get a new one for about $150."

"I know. You told me."

"Well, it's just that you can't always spend the night here."

"Don't worry about it," Carrie says. "The heat doesn't bother me."

"I don't want you to be hot. In your apartment," says Mr. Big.

"If you're only asking me over because you feel sorry for me, don't," Carrie says. "I only want to come over if you miss me. If you can't sleep without me."

"Oh, I'd miss you. Sure. Of course I'd miss you," Mr. Big says. And then after a few seconds: "Do you have enough money?"

Carrie looks at him. "Plenty," she says.

LOBSTER NEWBERT

There's something about this heat wave. It's loosening. You feel almost drunk, even though you're not. On the Upper East Side, Newbert's hormones are up. He wants to have a baby. In the spring, his wife, Belle, had told him she could never be pregnant in the summer, because she wouldn't want to be seen in a bathing suit. Now she says she could never get pregnant in the summer, because she doesn't want to have morning sickness in the heat. Newbert has reminded her that, as an investment banker, she spends her days behind the green glass walls of a coolly air-conditioned office tower. To no avail.

Newbert, meanwhile, spends his days puttering around the apartment in a ripped pair of boxer shorts, waiting for his agent to call with news about his novel. He watches talk shows. Picks at his cuticles with blunt instruments. Calls Belle twenty times a day. She is always sweet. "Hello, Pookie," she says.

"What do you think about the Revlon stainless-steel tweezers with the tapered ends?" he asks.

"I think they sound wonderful," she says.

One night during the heat wave, Belle has a business dinner with clients. Japanese. A lot of bowing and shaking hands, and then they all go off, Belle and five dark-suited men, to City Crab. Halfway through dinner, Newbert makes an unexpected appearance. He's already quite drunk. He's dressed like he's going camping. He decides to do his version of the Morris dance. He takes cloth napkins and stuffs them in the pockets of his khaki hiking shorts. Then, swinging napkins in both hands, he takes a few steps forward, kicks up one leg in front, takes a few steps backward, and kicks up the other leg behind. He also adds in a few side kicks, which, technically, are not part of the original Morris dance.

"Oh, that's just my husband," Belle says to the clients, as if this sort of thing happens all the time. "He loves to have fun."

Newbert pulls out a small camera and starts taking pictures of the clients. "Everyone say robster," he says.

CANNIBALS AT LE ZOO

Carrie is at this new restaurant, Le Zoo, having dinner with a bunch of people she doesn't really know, including the new "It" boy, Ra. The restaurant has about three tables, and it's overbooked, so everyone stands on the sidewalk. Someone keeps bringing bottles of white wine outside. Pretty soon there's a party on the street. It's the beginning of the heat wave, and people are nice: "Oh, I've been dying to meet you." "We have to work together." "We have to see each other more." Carrie is talking to everyone and not hating anyone. Not feeling like everyone hates her for a change.

Inside the restaurant, Carrie sits between Ra and his female manager. Someone from the *New York Times* keeps taking everyone's picture. Ra doesn't talk much. He stares a lot and touches his goatee and nods his head. After dinner, Carrie goes back to Ra's manager's house with the manager and Ra to smoke. It seems to be the right thing to do at the time, in the summer, in the heat. The smoke is strong. It's late. They walk her to a cab.

"We call this place the zone," the manager says. She's staring at Carrie.

Carrie thinks she actually knows what she's talking about, what this "zone" is, and why they're suddenly all in it together.

"Why don't you come and live with us in the zone?" Ra asks.

"I'd like to," Carrie says, meaning it but also thinking, I've got to get home.

She rides uptown, but before she gets home she says, "Stop the cab." She actually gets out and walks. She's still thinking, I've got to get home. The city is hot. She feels powerful. Like a predator. A woman is walking down the sidewalk a few feet in front of her. She's wearing a loose white shirt, it's like a white flag and it's driving Carrie crazy. Suddenly Carrie feels like a shark smelling blood. She fantasizes about killing the woman and eating her. It's terrifying how much she's enjoying the fantasy.

The woman has no idea she's being stalked. She's oblivious, jiggling along the sidewalk. Carrie envisions tearing into the woman's soft, white flesh with her teeth. It's the woman's own fault, she should lose weight or something. Carrie stops and turns into her building.

"Good evening, Miss Carrie," says the doorman.

"Good evening, Carlos," Carrie says.

"Everything okay?"

"Oh yes, everything's fine."

"Good night now," Carlos says, sticking his head around the open door of the elevator. He smiles.

"Good night, Carlos." She smiles back, showing all of her teeth.

THE BLUE ANGEL

In the heat, going outside is bad. But staying inside, alone, is worse.

Kitty is knocking around in the big Fifth Avenue apartment she lives in with Hubert, her fifty-five-year-old actor boyfriend. Hubert is making a comeback. He's shooting a film in Italy with a hot young American director, and then he's going to L.A. to shoot the pilot for a TV series. Kitty will join him in Italy in a couple of days and then go to L.A. with him. She thinks: I'm only twenty-five. I'm too young for this.

At five o'clock, the phone finally rings.

"Hello, Kitty?" It's a man.

"Yeeeees?"

"Is Hubert there?"

"Noooooo."

"Oh, this is Dash."

"Dash," Kitty says, somewhat confused. Dash is Hubert's agent. "Hubert's in Italy," Kitty says.

"I know," Dash says. "He told me to call you and take you out if I was in town. He thought you might be lonely."

"I see," Kitty says. She realizes he's probably lying, and she's thrilled.

They meet at the Bowery Bar at ten. Stanford Blatch eventually shows up. He's a friend of Dash's, but then again, Stanford is a friend of everyone's.

"Stanford," Dash says. He leans back against the banquette. "Where's the new place to go? I want to make sure my ward here has a good time this evening. I think she's bored."

The two men exchange glances. "I like the Blue Angel," Stanford says. "But then again, I have particular tastes."

"The Blue Angel it is," Dash says.

The place is in SoHo somewhere. They walk in, and it's a seedy joint with plywood platforms for dancing girls. "Slumming is very big this summer," Stanford says.

"Oh please. I've been slumming for years," says Dash.

"I know. You're the type of person who will be talking on his car phone and say, 'Could you hold on please? I'm in the middle of getting a blow job on the Palisades Parkway and I'm just about to come,'" Stanford says.

"Sunset Boulevard only," Dash says.

They sit down right in front of one of the platforms. In a little bit, a woman comes out. She's carrying a bouquet of daisies that looks like she plucked them out of a crack in the sidewalk. She's totally nude. She's also skinny with cellulite. "You know something's really wrong when you see a skinny girl with cellulite," Kitty says, whispering in Dash's ear.

Dash looks at her and smiles indulgently. Okay, I can handle this, Kitty thinks.

The woman grabs a feather boa and begins dancing. She plucks out the flower petals. She's totally sweaty. She lies down and rolls on the dirty platform, and when she gets up, she has bits of chicken feathers and ragged petals and dirt stuck all over her body. Then she opens her legs and thrusts herself toward Kitty's face. Kitty is certain she can smell the woman. But she thinks, Okay, I've survived this.

Then a dyke couple comes out. They perform. The little woman moans. Then the bigger woman starts choking her. Kitty can see the veins sticking out on the little woman's neck. She's really being strangled. I'm in a snuff club! Kitty thinks. Stanford orders another glass of white wine.

The big woman grabs the little woman's hair and pulls. Kitty wonders if she should try to do something. The woman's hair comes off, and it's a wig and underneath she has a fuchsia crewcut.

"Show's over," Dash says. "Let's go home."

Outside, it's still hot. "What the hell was that about?" Kitty asks.

"What else did you expect?" Dash says.

"Goodbye, Kitty," Stanford says smugly.

THE CRACKUP

By the tenth day of the heat wave, Carrie was too attached to Mr. Big. Way too attached. That was the night that she had her breakdown. It started fine: Mr. Big went out alone to a business dinner. No problem at first. She went to her girlfriend Miranda's. They were going to sit in the air conditioning and watch taped segments of *Ab Fab*. But then they started drinking. Then Miranda called her drug delivery guy. It continued from there. Carrie hadn't seen Miranda for a while because she'd been busy with Mr. Big, so Miranda started in on her.

"I'd like to meet him, you know. Why haven't I met him? Why haven't I seen you?" Then she dropped the bomb. Miranda said she knows some girl who was dating Mr. Big during the first month he was dating Carrie.

"I thought he only saw her once," Carrie said.

"Oh, no. They saw each other several times. Se-ver-al. That's why I didn't call you for a whole month. I didn't know whether to tell you or not."

"I think this is bad stuff," Carrie said.

The next morning, after the freakout, when Carrie was lying in Mr. Big's bed, she tried to think about what she really wanted. Life felt like it had changed, but had it really? She thinks: I'm still not married. I still don't have kids. Will it ever happen?

When?

It's the zone or Mr. Big, she thinks. The zone or Mr. Big.

That afternoon, Mr. Big sends her flowers. The card reads: "Everything will be okay. Love, Mr. Big."

"Why did you send me flowers?" Carrie asks him later. "That was so sweet."

"I wanted you to know that somebody loved you," Mr. Big says.

A couple of days later, on the weekend, Carrie and Mr. Big go to his house in Westchester, so Mr. Big can play golf. He leaves in the morning, early. Carrie gets up late, makes coffee. She goes outside and walks around the yard. She walks to the end of the street. Walks back. Goes back inside the house and sits down.

"Now what am I going to do?" she thinks, and tries to imagine Mr. Big on the golf course, swatting golf balls impossible distances.

18

How to Marry a Man in Manhattan—My Way

A couple of months ago, an announcement appeared in the *New York Times* that "Cindy Ryan" (not her real name) had gotten married. There was nothing particularly interesting or unusual about it, except to people who had known Cindy and lost contact with her, like me, to whom the news was astounding. Cindy had gotten married! At forty! It was nothing short of inspirational.

You see, Cindy was one of those New York women who had been trying to get married for years. We all know them. They're the women we've been reading about for the past ten years, who are attractive (not necessarily beautiful) and seem to be able to get everything—except married. Cindy sold advertising for a car magazine. She knew stereo equipment. She was as big as a man. She shot guns and traveled (once, on her way to the airport, she had to punch out a drunk cab driver, throw him in the back seat, and drive herself to the airport). She wasn't exactly the most feminine woman, but she always had men.

But every year, she got older, and when I would run into her at an old friend's cocktail party, she'd regale me and everyone else with stories of the big one who got away. The guy with the yacht. The famous artist who couldn't get a hard-on without having a paintbrush pushed up his bum. The CEO who came to bed in mouse slippers.

And, you couldn't help it. You'd look at her and feel a mixture of admiration and revulsion. You'd walk away thinking, She'll never get married. If she does marry, it's going to have to be some boring bank manager who lives in New Jersey. And besides, she's too old.

Then you'd go home and lie in bed, and the whole thing would come back to haunt you, until you had to call up your friends and be a nasty little cat and say, "Sweetie, if I ever end up like her, be sure to shoot me, huh?"

Well, guess what. You were wrong. Cindy got married. He's not the kind of guy she ever thought she'd end up with, but she's happier than she's ever been in her life.

It is time. Time to stop complaining about no good men. Time to stop calling your machine every half hour to see if a man has called. Time to stop identifying with Martha Stewart's lousy love life even if she is on the cover of *People* magazine.

Yes, it is finally time to marry a man in Manhattan, and best of all, it can be done. So relax. You have plenty of time. Martha, pay attention.

THREE CASHMERE SWEATERS

It's a fall weekend and it's raining. Carrie and Mr. Big are at the restaurant they go to in Bridgehampton. It's crowded, which is annoying, and the maître d' who always gives them a table isn't there. So she and Mr. Big are eating at the bar with their heads together. First, they were going to try this new thing that they'd tried on Mr. Big's birthday—ordering four entrees, like having Chinese food.

But Mr. Big wants to eat exactly the same thing Carrie is eating so they just end up having twin dinners.

"Do you mind?" Mr. Big says.

"No, I don't mind," Carrie says in the ridiculous baby voice they seem to use with each other practically all the time now. "Me too tired to care."

"Me too tired too," Mr. Big says, in the baby voice. His elbow brushes against her. Then he jabs her with it. "Beep beep," he says.

"Hey," she says. "Here's the line. Don't cross it."

"Sudden death," Mr. Big growls, leaning over and spearing her pasta with his fork.

"I'll give you sudden death," Carrie says.

"C'mon, hit me," he says, and she punches him in the arm and he laughs.

"Here you two are." They turn around and Samantha Jones is standing there with like three cashmere sweaters wrapped around her neck. "I thought you guys might be here," she says. Mr. Big says, "Uh huh." Sam and Mr. Big don't really get along. Once, when Sam asked why, Carrie explained it was because Sam always said mean things to her and Big didn't like it. Sam snorted and said, "I think you can take care of yourself."

Sam starts talking about movies, and Carrie has no choice— she has to start talking about movies, too. Mr. Big doesn't like to talk about movies. Carrie starts wishing Sam would go away so she could just talk to Mr. Big about their favorite new subject—moving to Colorado someday. She doesn't like herself for wishing Sam would leave, but sometimes when you're with a man that's the way it is, you can't help it.

DWEEBS, NERDS, AND LOSERS

"It was David P. that did it," Trudie said. Trudie is the editor in chief of a magazine for teenage girls. She is forty-one, but at times she looks like a lovely sixteen year old, with huge blue eyes and black hair.

She leaned back in her chair, pointed to a bookshelf crammed with photos. "I call that, 'Trudie and . . .'" she said.

"It's photos of me and all the losers I went out with. I like to catalogue things.

"I used to specialize in the two-year relationship. I did everything to make them work. Couples therapy. Talked for hours about commitment problems. Fought. And then I realized, you know what? I'm not going to change a forty-year-old guy who hates women. It's—not—my—problem.

"I set a deadline for myself. I said, I have to be married by the time I'm forty. I was dating David P. He was fifty and dishonest. I told him I wanted to be married. He kept making excuses. Sucking me back in. 'Let's just go on this one trip to China, and when we come back, we'll figure it out,' he'd say. And then we were in Venice, at the Gritti Palace, one of those rooms with the wooden shutters that open onto the Grand Canal. 'Let's face it,' he said. 'You're never going to find anyone in Manhattan who's going to want to get married. So why don't we just stay like this forever.' And that's when I left for good."

When Trudie got back to Manhattan, she dug out all her old Filofaxes and called every man she'd ever met in Manhattan. "Yes, every one of them: all the guys I'd passed over, who I'd thought were dweebs, nerds, losers, didn't have enough hair."

"My husband's name was on the list—he was the last one," Trudie said. "I remember thinking, If he doesn't work out, I don't know what I'm going to do." (This, of course, was typical New York–woman modesty, because New York women always know what they're going to do.) The truth is, Trudie had three dinners with her future husband (she didn't know he was going to be her husband then), and he went off to Russia for two months. It was the beginning of summer, and Trudie went to the Hamptons and completely forgot about him. In fact, she began dating two other guys.

Trudie smiled and examined her nails. "Okay, he called at the end of the summer, and we began seeing each other again. But the point is you have to be willing to walk at any time.

You have to put your foot down. They can't think you're this poor, suffering little woman who can't live without them. Because it's not true. You can."

When it comes to marrying a man in Manhattan, two rules apply. "You have to be sweet," said Lisa, thirty-eight, a correspondent for a network news show. But at the same time, said Britta, a photo rep, "you can't let them get away with anything."

For these women, age is an advantage. If a woman has survived single in New York until her mid- to late thirties, chances are she knows a thing or two about how to get what she wants. So, when one of these New York women targets a man as a potential husband, there is usually very little he can do to get away.

"You have to start the training from day one," said Britta. "I didn't know that I wanted to marry my husband at the beginning. I only knew that I wanted him, and I would do whatever it took to get him. And I knew I would.

"You can't be like these stupid girls who only want to marry rich guys," she continued. "You have to be a bit calculating. You always have to expect more than you have. Take Barry [her husband]. As much as he hated it, he didn't want a typical girl who would let him do whatever he wanted. If someone got him now, they'd be so lucky. He's smart, sweet, he cooks and cleans. And you know what? He hated it every step of the way."

Before Barry, Britta was the kind of woman who once made her date go to the coat check to get her a pack of cigarettes and ran out the back door with someone else while he wasn't looking. "I once called Barry from the top of a mountain in Aspen and cussed him out for ten minutes because he had another date for New Year's Eve. Of course, it was only a month after we'd met, but still."

After that, Barry pretty much came around, except for two slightly sticky problems. He liked to look at other women, and he sometimes complained about not having his space, especially after she moved in with him. "Well, first of all, I always made sure we had lots of fun," says Britta. "I cooked. We both gained thirty pounds. We got drunk together. We watched each other get drunk. We took care of each other when we puked.

"You have to do unexpected things. Like one time he came home and there were candles all over the place and I served him up a TV dinner. Then I used to make him put on some of my clothes. But you've got to watch these men all the time. I'm sorry, but they spend 80 percent of their time away from you. When they're with you, they can pay attention. Why should they be checking out some other chick when they're eating with you? One time, when Barry's eyes were wandering, I hit him over the head so hard he nearly fell off his chair. I told him, 'Put your tongue back in your mouth and your tail between your legs and finish your dinner.'"

Keeping him, however, is another story. "Women in this town don't care if a guy is married or engaged," Britta said. "They'll still go after him. You have to be on top of it all the time."

Sometimes Mr. Big seems to retreat into himself, and then there is only the surface Mr. Big. Friendly to everyone. Maybe affable is the word. Always perfectly turned out. White cuffs. Gold cufflinks. Matching suspenders (though he almost never takes his jacket off). It isn't easy when he's in that mode. Carrie wasn't always good with people she thought were too conservative. She wasn't used to it. She was used to everybody being drunk and doing drugs (or not doing them). Mr. Big got mad when Carrie said outrageous things like, "I'm not wearing any underwear," even though she was. And Carrie thought Mr. Big was too friendly to other women, especially models. They'd be out and a photographer would say, "Do you mind?" and then motion for Mr. Big to have his picture taken with some model, and it was insulting. One time a model sat on his lap, and Carrie turned and said, "Gotta go," with a really pissed-off look on her face.

"Hey, come on," Mr. Big said.

Carrie looked at the model, "Excuse me, but you're sitting on my boyfriend's lap."

"Resting. Just resting," the model said. "There's a big difference."

"You have to learn how to deal with this," Mr. Big said.

COMPARISON SHOPPING

Rebecca, thirty-nine, a journalist who got married last year, recalls a moment when she found another woman's phone number jumbled among her banker boyfriend's business cards.

"I called the number, and asked the bitch point-blank what was up," Rebecca said. Sure enough, the woman revealed that Rebecca's boyfriend had asked her out to dinner. "I hit the roof. I didn't scream at her, but I became like something out of one of those nighttime soap operas. I actually told her to keep her hands off and not to call him again. She said, 'You've got a great one there, you should be nice to him.' I said, 'Well, if he's so great, how come he called you when he's living with me?'

"Then I called him. He had the nerve to be livid with me for 'interfering in his private business.' I said, 'Get one thing straight, buddy. When you're going out with me, there is no private business.' Still, for about two days afterward, I thought we were finished. Then we got over it, and he asked me to marry him about three months later."

There are other methods. After Lisa had been seeing her future husband, Robert, for two months, he started to get squirmy.

"What do you think if I go out with other people?" he asked.

"I think you should do comparison shopping," Lisa said, supercoolly. "How else can you possibly appreciate me? I'm not a jailer."

That really blew him away.

"It's all about self-esteem," Lisa said. "Men have to feel that there are limits and you're not going to take anything."

One well-known problem is living with a guy before you're married, and then he doesn't do anything about asking you to marry him. This can be taken care of with dispatch. "Just heard a story," said Trudie. "Woman, living with guy for a year. One morning, she wakes up. 'Are we going to get married?' Guy says no. She says, 'Move out right now.' He asks her to marry him that weekend."

"One of the biggest mistakes women make is that they don't discuss marriage from the beginning," said Lisa.

I SHOULD LEAVE

I can't take it, Carrie thinks, waking up one morning. She lies there, watching Mr. Big until he opens his eyes. Instead of kissing her, he gets up to go to the bathroom. That's it, she thinks.

When he comes back to bed, she says, "Listen, I've been thinking."

"Yeah?" says Mr. Big.

"If you're not totally in love with me and crazy about me, and if you don't think I'm the most beautiful woman you've ever seen in your life, then I think I should leave."

"Uh huh," says Mr. Big.

"Really, it's no problem."

"Okay," Mr. Big says, somewhat cautiously.

"Soooooo . . . is that what you want?"

"Is it what you want?" says Mr. Big.

"No, not really. But I do want to be with someone who's in love with me," says Carrie.

"Well, I just can't make any guarantees right now. But if I were you, I'd hang around. See what happens."

Carrie lies back against the pillows. It's Sunday. It would be sort of a drag to have to go. What would she do with the rest of the day?

"Okay," she says, "but just for now. I don't have forever, you know. I'm probably going to die soon. Like in fifteen years or something." She lights up a cigarette.

"Okay," says Mr. Big. "But in the meantime, could you make me some coffee? Please?"

Naomi, who got married last year at thirty-seven, is the president of an ad agency and typical of most of us women in New York. "I dated every kind of man—all shapes and sizes. Then one day, the right guy walks in the door, and he was the antithesis of everything I always thought I wanted." In other words, he wasn't the proverbial bad boy.

When she was thirty-five, Naomi was waiting for a cab on Madison Avenue, dressed in a suit and high heels, and a long-haired guy zoomed by on a motorcycle and he didn't check her out. "Suddenly, the allure of the starving-tortured-artist type became passé," she said. "I was always paying for their goddamn dinners."

Carrie goes to a book party at a museum, and she brings Sam. She hasn't seen Sam for a while. She hasn't seen any of her girlfriends for a while because it seems like she spends all her time with Mr. Big. They're both wearing black pants and black patent leather boots, and as they get to the steps, Z.M., the media mogul, is coming down and getting into his car.

He laughs. "I was wondering who those two women were, stomping down the sidewalk."

"We weren't stomping," says Sam, "we were talking."

The driver was holding open the door of his limousine. "Call me sometime, huh?" he says.

"Call me," Sam says, and you know neither of them will. Sam sighs. "So, how's Mr. Big?"

Carrie starts hemming and hawing, going into her whole I-don't-know routine, they're planning to go to Aspen and he's talking about them getting a house together next summer, but she's not sure about him and . . .

"Oh, come on," Sam says. "I wish I had a boyfriend. I wish I could find someone I wanted to spend a weekend with, for Christ's sake."

There's one big difference in New York between women who get married and women who don't. "Basically, it's like, Get over yourself," Rebecca said. "Get over the idea that you should be marrying Mort Zuckerman."

"I narrowed it down to three qualities," Trudie said. "Smart, successful, and sweet."

They also never believe that they will not get married. "I always thought that it would take me however long it would take me, but it was going to happen," said Trudie. "It would be horrible if it didn't. Why shouldn't I be married?"

But Manhattan is still Manhattan. "The thing you have to realize is that, in terms of socialization for men, getting them ready for marriage, New York is a terrible place," Lisa said. "Single men don't tend to hang around with couples. They're not used to that idea of coziness and family. So you have to get them there mentally."

ELICIT COZINESS

Carrie and Mr. Big go to a charity event in an old theater, and they have a beautiful evening. Carrie has her hair done. It seems like she's having to have her hair done all the time now, and when she says to the stylist, "I can't afford to do this," he says, "You can't afford not to."

At dinner, Mr. Big swoops down on the table with his cigar and moves their place cards so they're sitting next to each other, saying, "I don't care." They hold hands the whole evening, and one of the columnists comes up and says, "Inseparable as always."

They have a good week after that, and then something tweaks in Carrie's brain. Maybe it's because they went to dinner at one of his friends' houses, and there were people there with kids. Carrie rode tiny plastic cars in the street with the kids, and one of the kids kept falling off her car. The parents came out and yelled at their kids to go back in the house. It didn't seem fair, because none of the kids got hurt.

She decides she has to torture Mr. Big again. "Do you think we're close?" she asks just before they're going to sleep.

"Sometimes," Mr. Big says.

"Sometimes isn't enough for me," she says. She continues to bug him until he begs her to let him go to sleep. But when she wakes up early the next morning, the bug is still there.

"Why are you doing this?" Mr. Big asks. "Why can't you think about the good things, like the way we were last week?"

He walks by the bed. "Oooh, look at that sad little face," he says, which makes her want to kill him.

"I'll talk to you about this later, I promise," Mr. Big says.

"I don't know if there's going to be any 'later,'" Carrie says.

Lisa was at a crowded party for a prominent publicist (we'll call her Sandy) in a town house in the East 50s. Lisa's husband, a handsome man who is in some kind of business, was in tow. In between sips of a pink margarita, she explained. "When I finally decided to look for someone, I thought about every place I'd ever met a man. It wasn't at Bowery Bar, it was at parties at people's houses. So I really spread the net. I went to every party at anyone's apartment.

"When you meet a guy, my rule is for the first few dates, no big parties. It's suicide. Do not be dressed up. Do not be on. Do not be working it, working the room. Men want to feel comfort. You must elicit coziness. Talk about the person they are, because most men's self-image is them at fourteen."

Back at her office, Trudie nodded at a large photo on her desk of a curly-haired man leaning against a dune on a beach. "My husband is such a find. He really understands me. When you find the right person, it's so easy. People who have a lot of fights and drama—well, something is wrong. My husband doesn't give me any argument. We never really fight about anything. He is so giving to me 99 percent of the time, on the few occasions when he wants his way, I'll give in."

And then suddenly everything is, weirdly, fine.

Mr. Big calls. "What are you doing?"

"Oh, you know, that thing I do sometimes," Carrie says. "Writing a story."

"About what?"

"Remember how we said that someday we'd move to Colorado and raise horses and shit? That's what I'm writing about."

"Oh," says Mr. Big. "It's a beautiful story."

19

Manhattan Psycho Moms Go Gaga for Goo-Goos

Mr. Big calls, only a little pissed off, from China. He'd sent his luggage via an express delivery service and now it's lost, and he's sitting in his hotel room with only a pair of jeans and a shirt and no clean underwear. "If this happened five years ago, someone would have been fired," he says. "But I've changed. It's the new me. If they can't deal with me in dirty jeans, fuck 'em."

"Guess what?" Carrie says. "Your friend Derrick called. He said Laura is trying to get pregnant and he doesn't want her to, so every night he pretends to come but doesn't, and then he goes into the bathroom and jerks off. And every night she's watching 'You and Your Baby' videos."

"What a wuss," says Mr. Big.

"And he says he can't do it because he's not far enough along in his career to afford a kid."

"And how about you?" Mr. Big asks, in his singsong way.

"Oh, I'm fine," Carrie says darkly. "I think I might be pregnant."

"A baby. We're going to have a baby," says Mr. Big.

Carrie isn't sure what to think.

You see, things happen to people when they have kids in New York. Some parents remain normal. But others, decidedly, do not. They go a little bit crazy. Take all that energy and aggression, those hangups and unresolved issues that go into one's career, and imagine applying them to a child. When it comes to kids, people who were once garden-variety New York City neurotics can become, well, just plain crazy.

That was evidenced immediately when Carrie went to brunch at the SoHo loft of her friends Packard and Amanda Deale. Packard and Amanda (normal) are the parents of Chester, who was marching around the loft banging an umbrella on the floor. One mother (not so normal) couldn't help but point out that he was "parallel-playing and not sharing, but it's okay, because he's only one, and no one expects him to share his toys—yet."

Like most couples who suddenly have children, the Deales have mysteriously taken on a whole new group of friends who also have kids. How does this happen? Did Packard and Amanda meet them at some early-admission nursery school gathering? Or were they always friends who, having kids, kept Amanda and Packard on the back burner until they caught up? The newfound friends include Jodi, who insisted that everyone give her only white baby clothes, because she believes that dye in clothing will cause an allergic reaction on her baby's skin; Suzanne, who won't let her nannies wear perfume because she doesn't want to come home and find her baby smelling of someone else's (cheap) cologne; and Maryanne, who kept firing babysitters, secretly on purpose, until she finally just had to quit her job to take care of the kid.

That kind of behavior is not limited to mothers. After all, isn't there something just a wee bit nutsy about fathers and sons who dress in identical Patagonia jackets with matching Rollerblade helmets? Or the father who, kissing his son repeatedly on the head in between holding his little mitts in his hand and dancing around the child's stroller (if it is possible for a two year old to look embarrassed, the kid does), explains, "All you have to do is have one of these and then take three or four years off."

Of course, being crazy about your kid and being just plain crazy are two slightly different things. Taken to extremes, there is only one word for a certain kind of New York parenting: psycho. You don't know who it will strike or what form it will take, but, said Packard, "It's not about love or caring; it's about obsession."

"ALEXANDRA!"

Carrie was sitting on the couch in the loft talking to a woman who appeared fairly ordinary. Becca had straight blond hair and the sort of long, thin nose that makes you think it could suck martinis out of a glass on its own. She'd just moved into a new apartment in the East 70s and was explaining the pros and cons of hiring a decorator—"One friend couldn't get this decorator to stop buying things, it was awful"—when suddenly she was interrupted by a five-year-old girl in a frilly dress and a black ribbon in her hair. "Mommy, I want the tit," demanded the child.

"Alexandra!" (Why is practically every kid named Alexander or Alexandra these days?) Becca said in a stage whisper. "Not now. Go and watch videos."

"But he's having titty milk," said the child, pointing to a woman who was nursing a baby in the corner.

"He's a baby. A little bitty baby," said Becca. "You can have juice."

"I don't want juice," Alexandra said. She actually had her hands on her hips.

Becca rolled her eyes. She stood and hauled the little girl onto her lap. The girl immediately started fussing with her mother's blouse.

"Are you still . . . breast feeding?" Carrie asked, as politely as possible.

"Sometimes," Becca said. "My husband wanted to have another child right away, and I didn't. It's so much work having a kid in New York. Isn't it, you little monster?" She gazed down at her child, who was now sucking her thumb, staring up at Mother, waiting for the unbuttoning. The child turned to Carrie, fixing her with an evil eye. "Titty milk. Titty milk," she said.

"Come on, Alexandra, I'll take you to the bathroom," said Becca. "We keep meaning to stop this now, don't we?"

The child nodded.

Becca wasn't the only mother at the party having problems getting an appropriate grip on her relationship with her child. Off in the bedroom, Julie, a small, dark-haired woman who manages a restaurant, was perched next to her six-year-old son, Barry. Barry is an adorable child, bearing an uncanny resemblance to his mother, with his dark curls. But he didn't look happy. He clung to Julie ferociously; when someone else tried to talk to her, he crawled all over her. "Oh, get off me. You're such a pain," Julie said to Barry, but she didn't really do anything about it. Barry won't play with the other children, nor will he let Julie talk to any adults. Later on, Carrie found out that it's always like this with the two of them—they go to parties, sometimes adult parties, and talk only to each other. She also learned that Julie keeps a mattress in Barry's room; most nights, she sleeps on the mattress. Julie's husband sleeps in the other room. They are planning on getting divorced.

"Well, that's pretty normal," said Janice, a corporate lawyer, who is one of the few psycho moms who has no problem admitting it. "I love my son," she said. "Andy is eleven months old. He is a god, and I tell him every day. The other day I found him in his crib saying, 'Me, me, me.'

"I was driven to have a baby since I was thirty," she continued. "So when I finally had him [she's now thirty-six], I was like, This is my calling in life. I'm a mom. I wasn't going to go back to work, but frankly, after three months, I knew

I had to go back to work. I'm in his face too much. In the park, I'm jumping up and down in front of him—the nannies think I'm crazy. I kiss him a thousand times a day. I can't wait to get home to give him a bath. His body makes me crazy. I never felt this way about any man."

Janice went on to say that if she sees Andy glance at another child's toy, she has to go out and buy it for him. One time she thought he was looking at something called the exersaucer. She finally found it on 14th Street, and she was running down 14th Street with it on her head because she couldn't get a cab and she couldn't wait to bring it home to him. "People were literally pointing at me on the street," she said. "Everyone thought I was insane. Then I get home and I give it to him and he starts crying."

Why is she like this? "It's something about New York," she said. She shrugged. "It's competitive. I want my son to have everything everybody else has, and more. Plus, I always wanted a boy. Sons always take care of their mothers."

THE NANNY CAMERA

In other words, after years of men who won't make commitments and can't be depended on, a son becomes a man substitute. "Oh, yeah," said Janice. "You can't trust men. You can't trust anyone who isn't your blood.

"My husband is really a second-class citizen," she said. "I used to be pretty crazy about him, but then the baby came along. Now, if he's like, 'Could you please get me a Diet Coke?' I tell him to buzz off."

Meanwhile, a small, wary crowd had gathered in the middle of the loft. Wobbling a bit was a tiny girl wearing pink ballet slippers and a tutu. "Brooke insisted on wearing her ballet outfit today. Isn't it adorable?" said a tall, beaming woman. "When I tried to put pants on her, she started crying. She knew. She knew she had to wear her ballet outfit today so she could put on a performance, didn't she, pumpkin? Didn't she, pumpkin?" The woman stooped, her hands clasped to her chest, her head cocked, and her face frozen in a large fake smile inches from the child's face. Then she began making odd gesturing motions.

"Blow a kiss. Blow a kiss," she said. The little girl, smiling fixedly, brought her little palm to her mouth and then whooshed out air between her lips. The mother screamed wildly.

"She curtseys, too," Amanda said with some derision to Carrie. "She does tricks. Her mother got Brooke on the cover of one of those baby magazines, and since then, she's gone nuts. Every time we call her, she's rushing Brooke off to a 'go-see.' She's with a modeling agency. I mean, she's cute, but . . ."

Just then, another mother walked by, holding the hand of a two-year-old boy. "Look, Garrick, table. Table, Garrick. Can you say table? What do we do at a table? Eat, Garrick. We eat at a table. Can you spell table? T-a-b-l-e. Garrick, rug. Garrick. R-u-g, rug, Garrick . . ."

Amanda started making onion dip. "Excuse me," said Georgia, a woman in a checked suit. "Onion dip? Just be sure to keep it away from the kids. The salt and fat makes them nuts." This sentiment, however, did not prevent her from dipping her finger into the heinous concoction and sticking it in her mouth.

"Hey, have you guys checked out the Sutton Gym?" Georgia asked. "It's fabulous. You have to take Chester to the Sutton. It's like a David Barton gym for kids. Has he started to talk yet? If he has, maybe we could make a playdate. Rosie is nearly one, but I want to start her on improving playdates.

"I also recommend the baby massage class at the 92nd Street Y. Very bonding. You're not still breast feeding, are you? I didn't think so." Georgia extracted another glop of onion dip. "Say, how's your nanny?"

"Fine," Amanda said, glancing at Packard.

"She's from Jamaica. We're lucky to have her," Packard said.

"Yeah, but are you sure she's taking good care of little Chester?" Georgia asked.

"He seems fine to me," Packard said.

"Yes, but I mean, good care," Georgia said, looking at Amanda meaningfully, at which point Packard slipped away.

"You can't be too careful with these nannies," Georgia said, leaning in toward Amanda. "I went through eleven nannies. Finally, I got the spy camera."

"Spy camera?" Carrie asked.

Georgia looked at Carrie as if seeing her for the first time. "You don't have kids, do you? Anyway, I thought it was going to cost a fortune, but it doesn't. This friend of mine saw it on *Oprah*. A guy comes to your house and sets it up. You can watch your nanny for five hours. I called mine and said, 'What did you do today?' She said, 'Oh, I took Jones to the park, then we played.' It was all a lie. She hadn't even left the house! All she did all day was watch TV and talk on the phone. She practically ignored Jones the whole day. I've got all my girl-friends doing it. One of them watched the nanny trying to dismantle the spy camera!"

"Wow," said Amanda.

I'm going to get sick, Carrie thought.

"MARRIED SEX"

Carrie went into the bathroom in Packard and Amanda's room. Julie was still in the bedroom with Barry. He was lying on the bed with his head in her lap. Becca and Janice were in there, too. Talking about their husbands.

"Let me tell you something about married sex," Becca said. "What's the point?"

"What's the point of a husband?" Julie said. "I mean, who needs two babies?"

"I totally agree," said Janice. "Except that now I want to have another baby. I was thinking of getting rid of my hus-band, but now I'm not sure that I want to—yet."

Julie leaned over her son. "When are you going to grow up, baby baby?"

Carrie went back into the living room. She walked over to the window for some fresh air. Somehow, Garrick had become detached from his mother and was standing, looking lost, in the corner.

Carrie leaned over. She took something out of her purse. "Pssst. Hey kid," she said, motioning. "Come here."

Curious, Garrick wandered over. Carrie held up a small, plastic package. "Condom, Garrick," she whispered. "Can you say condom? C-O-N-D-O-M. If your parents had used one of these, you might not even be here."

Garrick reached out for the plastic package. "Condom," he said.

Two days later, Amanda called Carrie. "I've just had the worst day of my life," she said. "My nanny has a kid—a son—three months older than Chester. Her kid got sick, so I had to stay home.

"First, I tried taking him to the park. I didn't know where the gate was to the playground, and I felt totally embarrassed because all of the other nannies were already inside and I couldn't figure out how to get in. They were all looking up at me like, Who are you? Then Chester wanted to go on the slide. Like twenty times. I kept looking up at the big clock on Fifth Avenue. Five minutes had passed. I swung Chester on the swing. Another five minutes. I let him play in the sandbox. Then more sliding. A total of fifteen minutes had passed. 'Haven't you had enough?' I said. I put him kicking and screaming into his stroller. 'We've got to run some errands,' I said.

"Poor Chester. I was racing him up the sidewalk, and he was bumping around in the stroller, not knowing what was going on. I tried to go shopping, but I couldn't get the stroller into the dressing room. Then we went to the bank, and the stroller got stuck in the revolving door. I mean, how am I supposed to know that you're not supposed to put a stroller in a revolving door? We were trapped. Some man had to push us through, inch by inch.

"Finally, it was eleven-thirty. I took him home and cooked him lunch. An egg."

Later that night, Carrie called Mr. Big. She forgot about the time difference—he was sleeping. "I just wanted to tell you," she said. "I got my period."

"Oh. So . . . no baby," he said.

They hung up, but two minutes later he called back.

"I just remembered the dream I was having," he said. "I dreamed we had a baby."

"A baby?" Carrie asked. "What kind of baby?"

"A little tiny one," said Mr. Big. "You know. A newborn. Lying right here in the bed with us."

When Mr. Big is Away,
the Girl Comes to Play

Carrie met the Girl in the bathroom stall at a club. She didn't mean to meet the Girl.

Someone was knocking on the door of the stall. Carrie was in a good mood, she was hanging out in the stall with Cici, so instead of telling the person to buzz off, she opened the door a crack. The Girl was standing there. She had dark hair and she could have been beautiful. "Can I come in?"

"Yeah, sure," Carrie said.

"Excuse me," Cici said, "but do we know you?"

"No, we don't," Carrie answered.

"What do you have?" the Girl asked.

"What do you want?" Carrie said.

"I've got some great weed," the Girl said.

"Good," Carrie said.

The Girl lit the joint and held it up. "Best weed you've ever smoked."

"I doubt it," Carrie said, inhaling deeply.

The club was crowded, and it was pleasant to be hanging out in the bathroom stall. The Girl leaned back against the wall and toked on the joint. She said she was twenty-seven, and Carrie didn't believe her, but that was okay, too. Because, at first, she was just a girl she met in the bathroom. It happened all the time.

"So, like, what do you do?" Cici asked.

"I'm developing my own skin care company," the Girl said.

"Ah," Carrie said.

"It's based on science. I'd love to take care of your skin for you."

"Oh, really?" Carrie said. She lit up a cigarette. Other people were banging on the door now.

"We should get out of here," Cici said.

"I'd like someone to take care of my skin," Carrie said. "I don't think it's quite as good as it could be."

"Let me out," Cici said.

"I can make it better," the Girl said.

She was on the short side, but she had presence. A cool face that could be beautiful, but you had to keep looking at it to make sure. She was wearing leather pants, boots. Both expensive. Her voice was low.

"There are people out there who know me," Cici said. She was fidgeting.

"Chill out," Carrie said.

"I want you to hang with me," the Girl said. "I want you to stay with me the whole night. I think you're beautiful, you know."

"Yeah, sure," Carrie said. But she was surprised.

WHAT'S WRONG WITH ME?

In eighth grade, Carrie knew a girl named Charlotte Netts. Charlotte was one of the popular girls, which basically meant she was an early developer. Charlotte used to invite other girls over to spend the night. She used to send notes to girls, too. Carrie's friend Jackie went to spend the night at Charlotte's, and the next day it turned out that she had called her father in the middle of the night to come get her. Charlotte, Jackie said, had "attacked" her. She tried to kiss her and touch her breasts, and she wanted Jackie to do the same thing to her. She said it was "practice for boys." After that, they weren't friends anymore.

It was a scary story, and for years, Carrie would never sleep in the same bed with other girls or undress in front of them, even though you were supposed to be able to do that, because it was just girls. She used to think, What is wrong with me, why can't I just be like everybody else and not be uptight about it? But it would be terrible to have to say no to sexual advances from someone who was your friend.

A few years back, two of her girlfriends had gotten drunk and ended up spending the night together. The next day, both of them called Carrie and complained about how the other one tried to have sex with her, and how Carrie had better watch out. Carrie didn't know which one to believe. But the two women were never friends again.

ROUGH PERSUASION

Mr. Big was away for the whole month of October, and everything was just a little bit off. On the streets on the Upper East Side, people were walking around in their fall clothing, but the weather was too warm and sunny. At first, Carrie stayed home nights, not drinking and reading Jane Austen's *Persuasion* instead of seeing the movie. She'd read it twice before, but this time the book was boring, the characters going on in long speeches, and Carrie was depressed from a lack of alcohol and parties. Then she tried going out, but no one had changed or was doing anything new.

One night, Stanford Blatch came late to Wax, the new nightclub in SoHo, with a man's handkerchief tied around his neck.

"What's up?" Carrie asked, and Stanford said, "Oh, you mean with this? It's the Goose Guy's fault." The Goose Guy was a man who liked to have his neck wrung during sex. "Which was fine," Stanford said, "until he tried it on me. Meanwhile, I'll probably see him again. That's how sick I am."

The next night, she had dinner with Rock McQuire, a TV actor. "I really want a boyfriend," he said. "I think I'm finally ready for a relationship."

"You're such a great guy," Carrie said. "You're smart, cute, really successful. You shouldn't have a problem."

"But it's not that easy," Rock said. "I don't want to go out with a twenty-two-year-old pretty boy. But if I go out with someone in their thirties, they have to be really successful, too. And how many guys are there around like that? So instead, I end up going to a sex club and having an encounter and going home. At least it's not, you know, emotionally messy."

The next morning, Miranda called up. "You'll never believe what I did," she said, and Carrie said, "What, sweetie?" while her right hand curled into a fist, a gesture she's been repeating a lot lately.

"Got a second? You're gonna love this."

"I don't, but I'm dying to hear it."

"I went to a party with my friend Josephine. You know Josephine, right?"

"No, but . . ."

"I introduced you. At that party that my friend Sallie had. You remember Sallie, don't you? Motorcycle Sallie?"

"Motorcycle Sallie."

"Right. There were all these baseball players there. And guess what? I made out with one of them, and then I went into a bedroom with another and we did it, right at the party."

"That's incredible," Carrie said. "Was it great?"

"Awesome," Miranda said.

Something's gotta give, Carrie thought.

BEHIND THE WALL

"Let's go to some clubs," the Girl said. They were sitting on a banquette. Carrie, the Girl, and the Girl's friends, who turned out to be unattractive guys in their twenties with short, frizzy hair. "They're richer than anyone you'll ever meet," the Girl whispered, earlier, but Carrie thought they were completely forgettable.

Now the Girl was pulling her arm, pulling her to her feet. She kicked the guy who was closest to her. "C'mon, asshole, we want to go out."

"I'm going to a party in Trump Tower," the guy said, with a fake Euro-accent.

"Like hell you are," she said.

"C'mon, sweetie. Come out with us," she whispered to Carrie.

Carrie and the Girl crammed into the front seat of the kid's car, which was a Range Rover, and they started going up-town. Suddenly the Girl yelled, "Stop the car, you shithead!" She leaned over and opened the door and pushed Carrie out. "We're going," she said.

And then they were two girls running down the streets west of Eighth Avenue.

They found a club and they went in. They walked all through the club holding hands and the Girl knew some people there and Carrie didn't know anyone and she liked it. Men looked at them, but they didn't look back. It wasn't like two girls going out looking for a good time; there was a wall up. On other side of the wall was freedom and power. It felt good. This is the way I'm going to be from now on, Carrie thought. It didn't feel scary.

Carrie remembered that at a party recently a woman named Alex told her a story about a friend of hers who was bisexual. She went out with women and men. She'd be with a man she liked, and then she'd meet a woman she liked and leave the man for the woman.

"I mean, I've never been with a woman," Alex said. "Maybe I'm the only one—but who hasn't said, 'I wish I could be a lesbian just so I wouldn't have to deal with men.' But the funny thing is, my friend said being with a woman was so intense because you're both women in the relationship. You know how women always want to talk about everything? Well, imagine that times two. It's constant talking. About everything, until four in the morning. After a while, she has to leave and go back to a man because she can't take the talking."

"Have you ever been with a woman?" the Girl asked Carrie. "You'll like it."

"Okay," Carrie said. She was thinking, I'm ready for this. It's time. Maybe I've secretly been a lesbian my whole life and I just didn't know it. She imagined the kissing. The Girl would be softer and squishier than a man. But it would be okay.

Then Carrie went back to the Girl's house. The Girl lived in an expensive high-rise, two-bedroom apartment on the Upper East Side. The furniture was that Danish stuff with knitted afghans. There were porcelain kittens on the side tables. They went into the kitchen and the Girl lit up a roach. She had a small, earthenware bowl filled with roaches. She had an open, half-empty bottle of wine. She poured them both some wine and handed Carrie a glass.

"I still sleep with men sometimes," the Girl said. "They just drive me crazy."

"Uh huh," Carrie said. She was wondering when the Girl was going to make her move and how she would make it.

"I sleep with men and women," the Girl said. "But I prefer women."

"Then why sleep with men?" Carrie asked.

The girl shrugged. "They're good for stuff."

"In other words, it's just the same old story," Carrie said. She glanced around the apartment. She lit up a cigarette and leaned back against the counter. "Okay," she said. "What's the deal? Really. You must be independently wealthy to be able to afford this place, or else you've got something else going on."

The Girl took a sip of her wine. "I dance," she said.

"Oh, I see," Carrie said. "Where?"

"Stringfellows. I'm good. I can make about a thousand a night."

"So that's what this is about."

"Can I have a cigarette?" the Girl asked.

"Topless dancers all sleep with each other because they hate men."

"Yeah, well," the Girl said, "the men are all losers."

"The ones you know. The ones who go into the club," Carrie said.

"Is there any other kind?" the Girl asked. In the kitchen light, Carrie saw that her skin was not so good, that it was pockmarked under a heavy coat of foundation. "I'm tired," the Girl said. "Let's go lie down."

"Let's do it," Carrie said.

They went into the bedroom. Carrie sat on the edge of the bed, trying to keep up a patter of conversation. "I'm going to get more comfortable," the Girl said. She went to her closet. She took off her fancy leather pants and put on sloppy gray sweatpants. She took out a T-shirt. When she undid her bra, she turned away. Without her clothes on, she was short and kind of chubby.

They lay down on top of the bed. The pot was beginning to wear off. "Do you have a boyfriend?" the Girl asked.

"Yes," Carrie said, "I do and I'm crazy about him."

They lay there for a few minutes. Carrie got an ache in her stomach from missing Mr. Big.

"Listen," Carrie said, "I've got to go home. It was great to meet you, though."

"Great to meet you," the Girl said. She turned her head to the wall and closed her eyes. "Make sure the door is shut on your way out, okay? I'll call you."

Two days later, the phone rang and it was the Girl. Carrie thought, Why did I give you my number? The Girl said, "Hi? Carrie? It's me. How are you?"

"Fine," Carrie said. Pause. "Listen. Can I call you right back? What's your number?"

She took down the Girl's number, even though she already had it. She didn't call back, and for the next two hours until she went out, she didn't answer the phone. She let the machine pick up.

CATWALK

A few days later, Carrie was at the Ralph Lauren fashion show in Bryant Park. The girls, tall and slim, came out one after another, their long blond hair floating over their shoulders. For a moment, it was a beautiful world, and when the girls passed, their eyes met and they gave each other secret smiles.

21

Women Who Ran with Wolves: Perennial Bachelors? See Ya

In the past few weeks, several seemingly unrelated yet similar incidents occurred.

Simon Piperstock, the owner of a software company, was lying in bed in his plush two-bedroom apartment, nursing the flu, when the phone rang.

"You piece of shit," said a woman's voice.

"What?" Simon said. "Who is this?"

"It's me."

"Oh. M.K. I was going to call you, but I got the flu. Terrific party the other night."

"I'm glad you enjoyed it," M.K. said. "Because nobody else did."

"Really?" Simon sat up in bed.

"It's you, Simon. Your behavior is reprehensible. It's disgusting."

"What did I do?" Simon asked.

"You brought that bimbo. You always bring a bimbo. No one can stand it anymore."

"Hey. Hold on a second," Simon said. "Teesie is not a bimbo. She's a very bright girl."

"Right, Simon," M.K. said. "Why don't you get a life? Why don't you get married?"

She hung up.

Harry Samson, forty-six, a well-known, eligible-bachelor art dealer, was having one of his typical drinking evenings at Frederick's, when he was introduced to a very attractive woman in her mid-twenties. She had just moved to New York to be an assistant to an artist with whom Harry worked.

"Hi. I'm Harry Samson," he said in his East Coast drawl, affected, perhaps, by the fact that he had a cigarette hanging from the corner of his mouth.

"I know who you are," the girl said.

"Have a drink?" Harry asked.

She glanced at the girlfriend who accompanied her. "You're that guy, aren't you?" she said. "No, thanks. I know all about your reputation."

"This place sucks tonight," Harry said to no one in particular.

There's something rotten in New York society, and it's the character formerly known as the "eligible" bachelor. It's not your imagination. Those men in their forties and fifties who have never been married, who have not, in years anyway, had a serious girlfriend, have acquired a certain, unmistakable stink. The evidence is everywhere.

Miranda Hobbes was at a Christmas party when she ran into Packard and Amanda Deale, a couple she had met briefly through Sam, the investment banker she had dated for three months over the summer.

"Where have you been?" Amanda asked. "We called you to come to a couple of our parties, but we never heard from you."

"I couldn't," Miranda said. "I know you're friends with Sam, and, I'm sorry, but to tell you the truth, I just can't stand him. I can't stand being in the same room with him. That man is sick. I think he hates women. He leads you on, tells you he wants to get married, and then doesn't call. Meanwhile, he's trying to pick up twenty-one year olds."

Packard moved closer. "We're not friends with him anymore, either. Amanda can't stand him, and neither can I. He's gotten to be friends with this guy named Barry, and all the two of them do every night is go to these SoHo restaurants and try to pick up women."

"They're in their forties!" Amanda said. "It's gross."

"When are they going to grow up?" Miranda asked.

"Or come out of the closet," Packard said.

CRYING NONWOLF

On a gray afternoon in late November, a man we'll call Chollie Wentworth was holding forth on one of his favorite topics— New York society. "These perennial bachelors?" he asked, ticking off the names of some well-known high rollers who have been part of the scene for years. "Frankly, my dear, they're just a bore."

Chollie tucked into his second Scotch. "There are a lot of reasons why a man might not get married," he said. "Some men never grow past sex; and for some people, marriage spoils sex. Then there's the difficult choice between a woman in her thirties who can bear you children, or a woman like Carol Petrie, who can organize your life.

"Mothers can also be a problem," Chollie continued. "Such is the case with X," he said, naming a multimillionaire financier who was now in his late fifties and had still not tied the knot. "He suffers from a permanent case of bimbo-itis. Still, if you're X, who are you going to bring home? Are you going to challenge your mother with a real standup woman who will disrupt the family?

"Even so," Chollie said, leaning forward in his chair, "a lot of people are tired of these guys' commitment problems. If I were a single woman, I'd think, Why bother with these guys, when there are 296 million amusing gay men out there who can fill a chair? I'd find a very amusing gay man who can be entertaining on a hundred topics to take me out. Why waste your time with X? Who wants to sit there and listen to him drone on about his business? To have to fawn all over him? He's old. He's too old to change. A man like X is not worth the effort. These men have cried nonwolf too many times.

"After all, it's women who decide if a man is desirable or undesirable. And if a man is never going to make the effort to get married, if he's never going to contribute . . . well, I think women are fed up. And for good reason."

JACK'S THANKSGIVING

"Here's what happens," said Norman, a photographer. "Take Jack. You know Jack—everybody knows Jack. I've been married for three years. I've known Jack for ten. The other day I'm thinking, In all the time I've known Jack, he's never had a girlfriend for more than six weeks. So we all go to a Thanksgiving dinner at some friends'. Everyone at the dinner has known each other for years. Okay, not everyone's married, but they're at least in serious relationships. Then Jack shows up, once again, with a bimbo. Twenty-something. Blond. Turns out, sure enough, she's a waitress he met the week before. So, one, she's a stranger, doesn't fit in, and changes the whole tenor of the dinner. And he's useless, too, because all he's thinking about is how he's going to get laid. Any time anyone sees Jack, it's this same scenario. Why spend time with him? After Thanksgiving, the women in our group all decided that Jack was out. He was banned."

Samantha Jones was having dinner at Kiosk with Magda, the novelist. They were discussing bachelors—Jack and Harry in particular.

"Someone said that Jack is still talking about who he scored with," said Magda. "It's the same conversation he was having fifteen years ago. Men think that a bad reputation is something that only women can get. They're wrong. Don't these guys understand that when you see who they want to be with—a bimbo—that you don't want to be with a man who wants to be with that?"

"Take a guy like Harry," Samantha said. "I can sort of understand Jack—he's totally into his career and making big money. But Harry doesn't want that. He says he doesn't care about power and money. On the other hand, he doesn't care about love and relationships, either. So exactly what is he about? What is the point of his existence?"

"Besides," said Magda, "who knows where these guys' dirty dicks have been."

"I couldn't find it less interesting," said Samantha.

"I ran into Roger the other day, outside Mortimers, of course," Magda said.

"He must be fifty now," Samantha said.

"Close to it. You know, I dated him when I was twenty-five. He'd just been named one of New York's most eligible bachelors by *Town & Country*. I remember thinking, It's all such a crock! First of all, he lived with his mother—okay, he did have the top floor of their town house, but still. Then there was the perfect house in Southampton and the perfect house in Palm Beach and the membership at the Bath & Tennis. And you know what? That was it. That was his life. Playing this role of eligible bachelor. And there wasn't anything below the surface."

"What's he doing now?" Samantha asked.

"The usual," Magda said. "He went through all the girls in New York, and when they finally got his number, he moved to L.A. From there, to London, now Paris. He said he was back in New York for two months, spending time with his mother."

The two women screamed with laughter.

"Get this," Magda said. "He tells me a story. 'I really like French girls,' he says. He goes to dinner at the home of this big shot Frenchman with three daughters. 'I'd take any of them,' he says. He's at dinner, he thinks he's doing pretty well, he tells them about his friend, some Arab prince, who has three wives, all of them sisters. The French girls start glaring at him, and the dinner ends almost immediately."

"Do you think these guys get it? Do you think they realize how pathetic they are?" Samantha asked.

"Nope," Magda said.

"I SUFFER"

The next day, Simon Piperstock made several calls from the first-class lounge at Kennedy International Airport. One of them was to a young woman he'd dated several years ago.

"I'm on my way to Seattle," Simon said. "I'm not good."

"Really." The woman sounded almost happy about it.

"For some reason, everybody is telling me that my behavior is reprehensible. They say it's disgusting."

"Do you think it's disgusting?"

"A little bit."

"I see."

"My relationship with Mary isn't working out, so I took a beautiful young girl, a friend of mine, to this party. She's a nice girl. And she's a friend. And everybody was on my case about it."

"Your relationships never work out, Simon."

"Then I ran into a woman at the theater who I'd been fixed up with a couple of years ago. And I wasn't really interested in her, so we became friends. She came up to me and she said, 'You know, I would never want to get involved with you. I would never want any of my friends to be involved with you. You've hurt too many women.'"

"You have."

"What am I supposed to do? I suffer from the problem of never thinking that I've met the right person. So I take people out. Jeez. Everybody's done it." There was a pause. "I was sick yesterday," Simon said.

"That's too bad," the woman said. "Did you wish you had someone to take care of you?"

"Not really," Simon said. "I mean, I was only sick for a little bit. . . . Damn it. Yes. It's true. I did think about it. Do you think I have a problem? I'd like to see you. Talk about it. Maybe you can help me."

"I have a serious boyfriend now," the woman said. "I think maybe we're going to get married. Frankly, I don't think he'd appreciate it if I was seen out with you."

"Oh," Simon said. "Okay."

"But if you want to call, feel free."

Bone and the White Mink: Carrie's Christmas Carol

Christmas season in New York. The parties. The star on 57th Street. The tree. Most of the time, it's never the way it should be. But once in a while, something happens and it works.

Carrie was at Rockefeller Center, thinking about ghosts of Christmas Past. How many years ago was it, she thought, putting on her skates, that I was last here? Her fingers trembled a little as she wrapped the laces around the hooks. Anticipation. Hoping the ice would be hard and clear.

Samantha Jones made her remember. Lately, Sam had been complaining about not having a boyfriend. About not having a love during the holidays for years and years. "You're lucky now," she told Carrie, and they both knew it was true. "I wonder if it will ever happen to me," Sam said. And both of them knew what "it" was. "I walk by Christmas trees, and I feel sad," said Sam.

Sam walks by Christmas trees and Carrie skates. And she remembers.

★ ★ ★

It was Skipper Johnson's second Christmas in New York, and he was driving everyone crazy. One night, he went to three cocktail parties in a row.

At the first one, he saw James, a makeup artist. James was at the second and third cocktail parties, too, and Skipper talked to him. He couldn't help talking to everyone. Remy, a hairstylist, came up to Skipper and asked, "What are you doing with that guy, James? You're too good for him."

"What do you mean?" Skipper said.

"I've seen the two of you everywhere together. And let me tell you something. He's scum. A user. You can do better."

"But I'm not gay," Skipper said.

"Oh, sure, darling."

The next morning, Skipper called up Stanford Blatch, the screenwriter. "People thinking I'm gay, it's bad for my reputation," he said.

"Please," said Stanford. "Reputations are like cat litter. They can be changed daily. In fact, they should be. Besides, I've got enough of my own problems right now."

Skipper called up River Wilde, the famous novelist. "I want to see-e-e you," he said.

"You can't," said River.

"Why not?"

"Because I'm busy."

"Busy with what?"

"With Mark. My new boyfriend."

"I don't get it," Skipper said. "I thought I was your friend."

"He does things for me that you won't do."

There was a pause.

"But I do things for you that he can't do," Skipper said.

"Like what?"

Another pause.

"That doesn't mean you have to be with him all the time," said Skipper.

"Don't you get it, Skipper?" River said. "He's here. His things are here. His underwear. His CDs. His hairballs."

"Hairballs?"

"He has a cat."

"Oh," Skipper said. Then: "You let a cat in your apartment?"

Skipper called up Carrie. "I can't stand it. It's Christmas, and everybody is in a relationship. Everybody except me. What are you doing tonight?"

"Big and I are staying home," Carrie said. "I'm cooking."

"I want a home," Skipper said. "I need a house. Maybe in Connecticut. I want a nest."

"Skipper," Carrie said, "you're twenty-five years old."

"Why can't everything be the way it was last year, when nobody was in a relationship?" Skipper moaned. "Last night, I had the most amazing dream about Gae Garden," he said, referring to the famously frosty socialite in her mid-forties. "She's so-o-o beautiful. And I had a dream that we were holding hands and we were so in love. And then I woke up, totally bummed because it wasn't true. It was just that feeling. Do you think you can ever have that feeling in real life?"

The year before, Skipper, Carrie, and River Wilde had all gone to Belle's Christmas party at her family's mansion in the country. Skipper drove his Mercedes, and River sat in the back seat like a papal personage and made Skipper keep flipping radio stations until he found some music he could tolerate. Afterward, they went back to River's apartment, and River and Carrie were talking while Skipper complained about how his car was parked illegally. Then Skipper went to the window and looked out, and sure enough, his car was being towed. He started screaming, and Carrie and River told him to shut up and do a line or smoke a joint or at least have another drink. And they thought it was hysterical.

The next day, Stanford Blatch went with Skipper to get his car out of the pound. The car had a flat tire, and Stanford sat inside the car, reading the papers, while Skipper changed the tire.

THE BONE

"I need a favor," Stanford Blatch said.

He and Carrie were having their annual Christmas lunch, at Harry Cipriani. "I have to sell some paintings in the Sotheby's auction. I want you to sit in the audience and bid them up."

"Sure," Carrie said.

"Frankly, I'm broke," Stanford said. After he lost his investment in a rock band, Stanford's family had cut him off. Then he'd gone through all the money from his last screenplay. "I've been such a fool," he said.

And then there was the Bone. Stanford had been writing a screenplay for him and paying for the Bone to get acting lessons. "Of course, he said he wasn't gay," Stanford said, "but I didn't believe him. Nobody understands. I took care of that kid. He used to fall asleep at night while we were talking on the phone. With the phone cradled in his arms. I've never met anyone who was so vulnerable. So mixed up."

The week before, Stanford had asked the Bone if he wanted to go to the Costume Institute benefit at the Met. The Bone freaked out. "I told him it would be good for his career. He screamed at me," Stanford said. "Insisted that he wasn't gay. That I should leave him alone. Said he never wanted to talk to me again."

Stanford took a sip of his Bellini. "People thought I was secretly in love with him. I thought I wasn't.

"He beat me up once. I was in his apartment. We got into a fight. I set up an audition for him with a director. He said he was too tired. That I should leave. I said, 'Let's talk about it.' He threw me against a wall, then he literally picked me up and threw me down the stairs. Of course he lived in a cheap walkup. A beautiful boy like that. My shoulder hasn't worked right since."

THE WHITE MINK

Carrie has been getting complaints about Skipper. From women who are older than he is. Like Carrie's agent, and one of her editors at a magazine. Skipper has been putting his hand on their knees under the table at dinners all over town.

The night of the Costume Institute benefit, Carrie was getting her hair done and yelling at Skipper on the phone when Mr. Big came home. He had a big package under his arm. "What's that?" Carrie asked.

"It's a present for me," Mr. Big said.

He went into the bedroom and came out holding a white mink coat. "Merry Christmas."

"Skipper, I have to go," Carrie said.

It was just three years ago Christmas that Carrie had been living in a studio apartment where an old lady had died two months before. Carrie had no money. A friend lent her a piece of foam for a bed. All she had was a mink coat and a Louis Vuitton suitcase, both of which were stolen when the apartment was inevitably robbed. But until then, she slept on the piece of foam with the fur coat over her, and she still went out every night. People liked her, and nobody asked questions. One night, she was invited to yet another party at someone's grand Park Avenue apartment. She knew she didn't really fit in, and it was always tempting to stuff your face on the free food, but you couldn't do that. Instead, she met a man who had a name. He asked her to dinner, and she thought, Fuck you, all of you.

They went to dinner at Elio's and sat at one of the front tables. The man laughed a lot and ate breadsticks spread with cold butter from his knife. "Are you a successful writer?" he asked.

"I have a story in *Woman's Day* next month," Carrie said.

"*Woman's Day*? Who reads *Woman's Day*?"

Then he said, "I'm going to St. Barts for Christmas. Ever been to St. Barts?"

"No."

"You should go. You really should. I rent a villa every year. Everyone goes to St. Barts."

"Sure," Carrie said.

The next time they had dinner, he had changed his mind and couldn't decide if he should go skiing in Gstaad or Aspen or to St. Barts. He asked her where she went to school.

"Nayaug High School," she said. "In Connecticut."

"Nayaug?" he asked. "Never heard of it. Hey, do you think I should get my ex-girlfriend a Christmas present? She says she's getting me one. Anyway."

Carrie just looked at him.

Still, her misery lifted for a few days until she realized that maybe he wasn't going to call again.

Two days before Christmas, she called him. "Oh, I'm about to take off," he said.

"Where did you decide to go?"

"St. Barts. After all. We've got a terrific house party. Jason Mould, the movie director, and his girlfriend, Stelli Stein, are coming in from L.A. But you have a very merry Christmas, okay? I hope Santa is good to you."

"You have a good Christmas, too," she said.

HI, MOM

That afternoon, she went ice skating, doing one spin after another in the center of the rink until they made everyone get off because the session was over. She called her mother. "I'm coming home," she said. It began snowing. She got on a train at Penn Station. There were no seats. She stood in the vestibule between the cars.

The train went through Rye and Greenwich. The snow turned into a blizzard. They passed Greens Farms and Westport and then the dirty little industrial towns. The train stopped, delayed because of the snow. Strangers began talking. It was Christmas.

Carrie lit a cigarette. She kept thinking about the man and Jason Mould and Stelli Stein (whoever she was) lying around a pool underneath a blue St. Barts sky. Stelli Stein would be wearing a white bikini and a black hat. They'd be sipping drinks through straws. People would come for lunch. And everyone would be long and tan and beautiful.

Carrie watched the snow blow into the car through a crack in the door. She wondered if she would ever get anything right.

It was midnight. Skipper was sitting in his apartment, talking on the phone to California, standing in front of the window. A cab pulled up to the building across the street. He could see a man and a woman in the back seat, making out. Then the woman got out, and she was wearing a big fur coat with like twelve cashmere sweaters wrapped around her head, and the cab drove off.

It was Samantha Jones.

Two minutes later, his doorbell rang.

"Sam," Skipper said. "I've been expecting you."

"Oh, please, Skipper. Stop with the juvenilities. I was wondering if I could borrow some shampoo," she said.

"Shampoo? How about a drink?" Skipper asked.

"A small one," Sam said. "And don't get any funny ideas. Like putting Ecstasy in it or anything."

"Ecstasy? I don't even do drugs. I've never even done coke, I swear. Wow. I can't believe you're in my apartment."

"I can't either," Sam said. She began walking around the living room. Touching things. "You know, I'm not quite as organized as everyone thinks."

"Why don't you take off your coat?" Skipper said. "Sit down. Do you want to have sex?"

"I really want to wash my hair," Sam said.

"You can wash it here," Skipper said. "After."

"I don't think so."

"Who was that man you were kissing in the cab?" Skipper asked.

"Just another man I either don't want or can't have," Samantha said. "Like you."

"But you can have me," Skipper said. "I'm available."

"Exactly," Sam said.

YOU'RE SO NAUGHTY

"Cheri," said a man's voice from the living room. "I'm so glad you come to see me."

"You know I always come to see you," said the Bone.

"Come here. I have some presents for you."

The Bone checked himself in the mirror in the marble foyer, then went into the living room. A middle-aged man was sitting on the couch, sipping tea, tapping his Italian-slippered foot against the coffee table.

"Come to me. Let me see you. See how you've aged in the past two months. No sun damage from our time in the Aegean?"

"You haven't aged at all," said the Bone. "You always look young. What's your secret?"

"That wonderful face cream you gave me," said the man. "What was it again?"

"Kiehl's." The Bone sat on the edge of a bergère.

"You must bring me some more," the man said. "Do you still have the watch?"

"The watch?" the Bone said. "Oh, I gave that to some homeless man. He kept asking me what time it was, so I figured he needed it."

"Oh! You're so naughty," the man said. "Teasing me like that."

"Would I ever give away anything you gave me?"

"No," the man said. "Now look at what I brought you. Cashmere sweaters in every color. You'll try them on?"

"As long as I get to keep all of them," the Bone said.

RIVER'S PARTY

River Wilde's annual Christmas party. Loud music. People everywhere. In the stairwell. Doing drugs. Someone was peeing off the balcony onto the head of the unsuspecting superintendent below. The Bone was ignoring Stanford Blatch, who showed up with twin male models who had just come into town. Skipper was making out with a woman in the corner. The Christmas tree fell over.

Skipper broke free and came up to Carrie. She asked him why he was always trying to kiss women. "I feel like it's my duty," he said, then asked Mr. Big, "Aren't you impressed with how fast I moved?"

Skipper moved on to River. "How come you never include me anymore? I feel like all my friends are dissing me. It's because of Mark, isn't it? He doesn't like me."

"If you keep this up, no one is going to like you," River said. Someone was puking in the bathroom.

At one A.M., the floor was awash in alcohol, and a cadre of druggies had taken over the bathroom. The tree had fallen over three times and no one could find their coat.

Stanford said to River, "I've finally given up on the Bone. I've never been wrong before, but maybe he really is straight." River stared at him, dazed.

"Come, River," Stanford said, suddenly happy. "Look at your Christmas tree. Look at how beautiful it is."

23

Party Girl's Tale of Sex and Woe: He Was Rich, Doting, and . . . Ugly

Carrie was walking out of Bergdorf's when she ran into Bunny Entwistle.

"Sweetie!" Bunny said. "I haven't seen you for years. You look great!"

"You, too," Carrie said.

"You must have lunch with me. Immediately. Amalita Amalfi—yes, she's in town too, and we're still friends—stood me up."

"Probably waiting for a phone call from Jake."

"Oh, is she still seeing him?" Bunny tossed her white-blond hair over the shoulder of her sable coat. "I have a table at '21.' Please have lunch with me. I haven't been in New York for a year, and I'm dying to dish."

Bunny was fortyish, still beautiful, L.A.-tanned, a sometime TV actress, but before that, she'd been around New York for years. She was the quintessential party girl, a girl so wild no man would consider marrying her, but plenty tried to get in her pants.

"I want a table in the back. Where I can smoke and no one will bother us," Bunny said. They sat down and she lit up a Cuban cigar. "The absolutely first thing I want to talk about is that wedding announcement." She was referring to a notice about the marriage of Chloe—thirty-six, still considered a classic beauty—to a homely fellow named Jason Jingsley in a ceremony on the Galápagos Islands.

"Well, he is rich, smart, and sweet," Carrie said. "He was always friendly to me."

"Please, darling," Bunny said. "Men like Jingles, and there's a whole group of them in New York, are not the type of guys you marry. They make great friends—attentive, always there when you're in a tight spot—and late at night when you're lonely and desperate as hell, you whisper to yourself, 'Well, I could always marry a guy like Jingles. At least that way I wouldn't have to worry about paying the rent.' But you wake up and really think about it, and realize that you'd have to share a bed with him, watch him brush his teeth, that stuff."

"Sandra said he tried to kiss her once," Carrie said. "She said, 'If I wanted a fur ball in my bed, I'd get a cat.'"

Bunny snapped open a compact, pretending to check her eyelashes but really, Carrie thought, checking to see if anyone in the restaurant was looking at her. "I'd love to call Chloe and ask her about it directly, but I can't, because she hasn't exactly been talking to me for years," she said. "Strangely enough, I did get one of those invitations to one of those Upper East Side museum benefits, and sure enough, Chloe is once again a cochair. I haven't gone to that benefit for years, but I actually thought about paying the $350 and going by myself. Just so I could see what she looked like."

Bunny laughed her famous laugh, and several heads swiveled around to look at her. "A few years back, when I was kind of fucked up and sometimes even had dried coke residue around my nostrils, my father used to call me up and say, 'Come home.' 'Why?' I'd ask. 'So I can seeeee you,' he'd say. 'If I seeeeee you I'll know whether or not you're all right.'

"It's the same thing with Chloe. If I can just see her, I'll know everything. Is she filled with self-loathing? Is she on Prozac?"

"I don't think so," Carrie started to say.

"Or do you think she's had some kind of remarkable religious experience?" Bunny continued. "People do these days. It's very chic.

"Anyway, I have my reasons for wanting to know. A few years ago, I almost married a guy like Jingles," Bunny said, slowly. "The situation is still not resolved and probably never will be.

"Let's have champagne. Waiter!" Bunny snapped her fingers. She took a breath. "Well. It all started after a nasty breakup with a man I'll call Dominique. He was an Italian banker, Euro-trashy and proud of it, with a personality like a scorpion. Just like his mother. Of course he treated me like shit and I put up with it, and strangely enough, I didn't mind that much. At least, not until the end when I drank too much psychedelic mushroom tea in Jamaica and realized he didn't love me after all. But I was a different person back then. I still had my beauty—you know, strangers stopped me on the street, that kind of thing—and a good-girl upbringing that comes from growing up in a small town in Maine. But on the inside, I was not nice. I had absolutely no feelings at all, emotionally or physically. I'd never been in love.

"The only reason I lived with Dominique for three years was, one, he asked me to on our first date, and two, he had a gorgeous two-bedroom apartment in a prewar overlooking the East River and a big house in East Hampton. I had no money, no job—I did some voice-overs and sang some jingles for TV commercials.

"So when Dominique and I broke up—he found out I was having affairs and made me give back jewelry he'd bought for me—I decided that what I needed to do was get married. Quickly."

THE TRILBY HAT

"I moved into a friend's apartment," said Bunny, "and about two weeks later I met Dudley at Chester's—that East Side bar for young swells. Within five minutes of meeting him, I was annoyed. He was wearing spectator shoes, a trilby hat, and a Ralph Lauren suit. His lips were damp. He was tall and skinny, with no chin to speak of, eyes like boiled eggs, and a large, bobbing Adam's apple. He sits down, uninvited, at our table, and he insists on ordering martinis for everyone. He tells bad jokes, makes fun of my pony-skin designer shoes. 'I'm a cow, moo, wear me,' he said. 'Excuse me, but I believe you're the big beef,' I said. I was embarrassed to be seen talking to him.

"The next day, sure enough, he called. 'Shelby gave me your number,' he said. Shelby's a friend of mine and somehow related to George Washington. I can be rude, but only up to a point. 'I didn't know you knew Shelby,' I said. 'Su-u-re,' he said. 'Since kindergarten. Even back then he was a goofy kid.'

"'He was? What about you?' I said.

"My mistake. I should never have gotten started with him. Before I knew it, I was telling him all about my breakup with Dominique, and the next day, he sent flowers 'because a beautiful girl shouldn't be depressed about being dumped.' Shelby called. 'Dudley's a great guy,' he said.

"'Yeah?' I said. 'What's so great about him?'

"'His family owns half of Nantucket.'

"Dudley was persistent. He sent gifts—stuffed bears and, one time, a Vermont cheese basket. He called three or four times a day. At first, he set my teeth on edge. But after a while, I got used to his bad sense of humor and almost looked forward to his calls. He listened with fascination to any spoiled, mundane detail of my day: you know, like how I was pissed because Yvonne had bought a new Chanel suit and I couldn't afford one; how a taxi driver kicked me out of the cab for smoking; how I cut my ankle again shaving. He was setting a trap for me and I knew it—but I still thought that I, of all people, could get out of it.

"And then came the weekend invitation, via Shelby, who called me and said, 'Dudley wants us to go to his house in Nantucket with him.'

"'Not on your life,' I said.

"'His house is beautiful. Antique. Main Street.'

"'Which one?' I asked.

"'I think it's one of the brick ones.'

"'You think?'

"'I'm pretty sure. But every time I was there, I was fucked up. So I don't really remember.'

"'If it's one of the brick houses, I'll think about it,' I said.

"Ten minutes later, Dudley himself called. 'I already bought your plane tickets,' he said. 'And yeah, it's one of the brick houses.'"

DUDLEY DANCES

"I still have no explanation for what happened that weekend. Maybe it was the alcohol, the marijuana. Or maybe it was just the house itself. As a kid, my family had spent summers on Nantucket. I say that, but the reality is, we spent two weeks at a rooming house. I shared a room with my brothers, and my parents boiled lobsters for dinner on a hot plate.

"I slept with Dudley that weekend. I didn't want to. We were on the landing of the staircase, saying good night, when he sort of swooped down and started to kiss me. I didn't refuse. We went to his bed, and as he lay on top of me, I remember at first feeling that I was being suffocated, which probably wasn't in my imagination since Dudley is six feet, two inches, and then feeling like I was sleeping with a little boy, since he couldn't have weighed more than 160 pounds and he had no hair on his body whatsoever.

"But for the first time in my life, the sex was great. I had a sort of epiphany: Maybe if I was with a guy because he was nice and adored me, I would be happy. But still I was afraid to look at Dudley when we woke up, afraid that I'd be repulsed.

"Two weeks after we got back to the city, we attended an Upper East Side museum benefit. It was our first official event together as a couple. And, in what would become typical of our relationship, it was a series of mishaps. He was an hour late, then we couldn't find a cab because it was 105 degrees. We had to walk, and Dudley—as usual—hadn't eaten anything that day and nearly passed out, and someone had to get him glasses of ice water. Then he insisted on dancing, which basically consisted of flinging me into other couples. Then he smoked a cigar and threw up. Meanwhile, everyone kept telling me what a great guy he was.

"Except my friends. Amalita said, 'You can do better. This is ridiculous.'

"I said, 'But he's great in bed.'

"She said, 'Please don't make me puke.'

"A month later, Dudley unofficially asked me to marry him, and I said yes. I had this feeling of shame about Dudley, but I kept thinking I would get over it. Plus, he kept me busy. We were always shopping. For apartments. Engagement rings. Antiques. Oriental rugs. Silver. Wine. And then there were weekend trips to Nantucket, and trips to Maine to visit my parents, but Dudley was perniciously late and always unorganized, so that we were always missing trains and ferries.

"The turning point came the night we missed a ferry to Nantucket for the fourth time. We had to spend the night at a motel. I was starving and wanted Dudley to go out and get Chinese food, but instead he came back with a head of iceberg lettuce and a pitiful looking tomato. While I lay in bed, trying to block out the noise of a couple screwing in the next room, Dudley sat at a Formica table in his boxers, cutting away the rotten parts of the tomato with his silver Tiffany Swiss Army knife. He was only thirty, but he had the persnickety habits of a seventy-five year old.

"The next morning, I started in. 'Don't you think you should work out? Gain a little weight?'

"After that, everything about him began to drive me crazy. His silly, flashy clothing. The way he acted like everyone was his best friend. The three long blond hairs on his Adam's apple. His smell.

"Each day, I tried to get him to the gym. I would stand there and force him to do reps with five-pound barbells, which was all he could handle. He actually did gain ten pounds, but then he lost it all again. One night, we went to dinner at his parents' apartment on Fifth Avenue. The cook was making lamb chops. Dudley insisted that he couldn't eat meat, screamed at his parents for not being considerate about his eating habits, and made the cook run out to the store to buy brown rice and broccoli. The dinner was two hours late, and still Dudley only picked at his food. I was mortified. Afterward, his father said to me, 'You come to dinner again anytime you like, but leave Dudley behind.'

"I should have ended it right there, but Christmas was two weeks away. On Christmas Eve, Dudley officially asked me to marry him, with an eight-carat ring, in front of my whole family. There was always something a little bit nasty about him, and in typical Dudley fashion, he squished the ring into a Godiva chocolate and then handed me the box. 'Here's your Christmas present,' he said. 'Better start eating.'

"'I don't want chocolates now,' I said, giving him the sort of dirty look that usually shut him up.

"'I think you do,' he said, somewhat menacingly, so I began eating. My family watched, in horror. I could have chipped a tooth, or worse, choked. Still, I said yes.

"I don't know if you've ever been engaged to the wrong person, but, once it happens, it's like being on a freight train

you can't stop. There were the rounds of Park Avenue parties, little dinners at Mortimers and Bilboquet. Women I hardly
knew had heard about the ring and begged to see it. 'He's
such a great guy,' everyone said.

"'Yes, he is,' I'd reply. And inside, I felt like a shitheel.

"And then the day came when I was supposed to move
into our newly bought, perfectly furnished classic-six apartment on East 72nd Street. My boxes were packed, and the
movers were downstairs when I called Dudley.

"'I can't do this,' I said.

"'Can't do what?' he asked.

"I hung up.

"He called back. He came over. He left. His friends called.
I went out and went on a bender. Dudley's Upper East Side
friends sharpened their knives. They made stuff up: I was
spotted at someone's house at four in the morning wearing
only cowboy boots. I'd given another guy a blow job at a
club. I was trying to pawn the engagement ring. I was a gold
digger. I'd taken Dudley for a ride.

"There is no good way to end these things. I moved into
a tiny studio apartment in a dirty walkup on York Avenue,
which I could actually afford myself, and started working on
my career. Things got worse for Dudley. The real estate
market crashed, and he couldn't sell the apartment. It was all
my fault. Dudley left town. Moved to London. Also, my fault.
Even though I kept hearing about what a great time he was
having. Dating some duke's homely daughter.

"Everyone forgets that the three years after that were hell
for me. Pure hell. Even though I had no money and had to
eat hot dogs on the street and was suicidal half the time—I
once actually called the suicide hot line, but then someone
beeped in inviting me to a party—I vowed I'd never get into
that situation again. Never take another penny from any man.
It's terrible to hurt someone like that."

"But do you really think it was because of the way he
looked?" Carrie asked.

"I've been thinking about that. And the one thing I forgot to mention is that every time I got into the car with him, I fell asleep. I literally couldn't keep my eyes open. The truth is, he bored me."

Maybe it was all the champagne, but Bunny laughed a little uncertainly. "Isn't that just awful?" she said.

24

Aspen

Carrie went to Aspen by Lear jet. She wore the white mink coat, a short dress, and white patent leather boots. It seemed like the thing to wear on a Lear jet, but it wasn't. The other people she was traveling with, the ones who owned the jet, were wearing jeans and pretty embroidered sweaters and sensible boots for snow. Carrie was very hung over. When the jet stopped for refueling in Lincoln, Nebraska, she had to be helped down the steps by the pilot. It was slightly warm, and she wandered around in her big mink and sunglasses, smoking cigarettes and staring out at the endless, flat, yellow-dry fields.

Mr. Big was waiting at the airport in Aspen. He was sitting outside, too perfectly dressed in a brown suede coat and a brown suede hat, smoking a cigar. He walked across the tarmac and the first thing he said was, "The plane is late. I'm freezing."

"Why didn't you wait inside?" Carrie asked. They drove through the tiny town, which was like a toy town lovingly placed by a child at the base of a Christmas tree. Carrie pressed her fingers over her eyes and sighed. "I'm going to relax. Get healthy," she said. "Cook."

Stanford Blatch also arrived by private jet. He was staying with his childhood friend Suzannah Martin. After River Wilde's party, he had told Suzannah, "I want to turn over a new leaf. We're such good friends, we should really think about getting married. That way, I can get my inheritance, and with your money and my money combined, we can live the way we've always wanted."

Suzannah was a forty-year-old sculptress who wore dramatic makeup and large pieces of jewelry. She had never seen herself in a traditional marriage anyway. "Separate bedrooms?" she asked.

"Naturally," Stanford said.

Skipper Johnson flew in commercial, upgrading his ticket to first class using mileage. He was vacationing with his parents and his two younger sisters. I have to find a girlfriend, he thought. This is ridiculous. He envisioned the lucky woman as older, somewhere between thirty and thirty-five, smart, beautiful, and lots of fun. Someone who could keep his interest. In the last year, he'd realized that girls his age were boring. They looked up to him too much, and it was scary.

Mr. Big taught Carrie to ski. He had bought her a ski suit, gloves, hat, long underwear. Also a tiny thermometer that clipped to her ski gloves—the one thing she had begged him to buy her. He had resisted until she pouted; then he agreed to buy it in exchange for a blow job even though it only cost four dollars. In the house they rented, he zipped up her ski suit, and she held out her hands and he put on her gloves. He clipped on the mini thermometer and she said, "You're going to be so glad we have this. It's cold out there." He laughed and they kissed.

Mr. Big smoked cigars on the gondola and talked on his cellular phone. Then he would ski behind Carrie on the slopes, watching to make sure no one ran into her. "You can handle it," he'd say, as she made turn after turn, curving slowly down the mountain. Then she'd stand at the bottom of the slope, shielding her eyes with her hand as she watched Mr. Big bounce over the moguls.

In the evenings, they would get massages and go in the hot tub. At night, when they were lying in bed together, Mr. Big said, "We're close now, aren't we?"

"Yes," Carrie said.

"Remember how you always used to say we had to be closer? You don't say that anymore."

Carrie thought, Things can't get any better.

"I'M LOOKING FOR TAIL"

Stanford Blatch was strolling along the top of Aspen mountain in a pair of pony-skin après ski boots and swinging a pair of binoculars, on his way to meet Suzannah at the lodge for lunch, when he heard a familiar voice scream out, "Stanford!" followed by "Watch out!" He turned just as Skipper Johnson was about to ski into him and deftly jumped back into a snow bank to avoid being hit. "Dear, dear Skipper," he said.

"Don't you love running into your friends on vacation?" Skipper asked. He was dressed in a ski suit that resembled what a Boy Scout might wear for inclement weather: Floppy yellow ski jacket and a hat with earflaps that stuck out at right angles.

"That depends on the friends and how one runs into them," Stanford said.

"I didn't know you were a bird watcher," Skipper said.

"I'm not looking for birds, I'm looking for tail," Stanford said. "I'm checking out the private jets so I'll know what kind to buy."

"You're getting a jet?" Skipper asked.

"Soon," Stanford said. "I'm thinking about getting married and I want to be sure my wife gets around properly."

"Your wife?"

"Yes, Skipper," Stanford said patiently. "In fact, I'm on my way to have lunch with her right now. Would you like to meet her?"

"I can't believe this," Skipper said. "Well," he said, snapping off his skis, "I've already hooked up with three different girls. Why not you?"

Stanford looked at him pityingly. "Dear, dear Skipper," he said. "When are you going to stop pretending you're straight?"

Carrie and Mr. Big went for a romantic dinner at the Pine Creek Cookhouse. They drove through the mountains, and then they took a horse-drawn sleigh to the restaurant. The sky was black and clear, and Mr. Big talked all about the stars, and how he was poor as a kid and had to leave school at thirteen and work and then go into the air force.

They brought a Polaroid camera and took pictures of each other in the restaurant. They drank wine and held hands and Carrie got a little drunk. "Listen," she said. "I have to ask you something."

"Shoot," said Mr. Big.

"You know at the beginning of the summer? When we'd been seeing each other for two months and then you said you wanted to date other people?"

"Yeah?" Mr. Big said cautiously.

"And then you dated that model for a week? And when I ran into you, you were horrible and I screamed at you and we had that big fight in front of Bowery Bar?"

"I was afraid you were never going to talk to me again."

"I just want to know," Carrie said. "If you were me, what would you have done?"

"I guess I never would have talked to you again."

"Is that what you wanted?" Carrie asked. "Did you want me to go away?"

"No," Mr. Big said. "I wanted you to stick around. I was confused."

"But *you* would have left."

"I didn't want you to go. It was like, I don't know. It was a test," he said.

"A test?"

"To see if you really liked me. Enough to stick around."

"But you really hurt me," Carrie said. "How could you hurt me like that? I can never forget that—you know?"

"I know, baby. I'm sorry," he said.

When they got back to their house, there was a message on the answering machine from their friend Rock Gibralter, the TV actor. "I'm here," he said. "Staying with Tyler Kydd. You guys will love him."

"Is that Tyler Kydd, the actor?" Mr. Big asked.

"Sounds like it," Carrie said, aware that she was trying to sound as if she couldn't have cared less.

PROMETHEUS BOUND

"That was just wonderful," Stanford said. He and Suzannah were sitting on the couch in front of the fire. Suzannah was smoking a cigarette. Her fingers were slim and elegant, ending in long, perfectly manicured red nails. She was wrapped in a black silk Chinese robe. "Thank you, darling," she said.

"You really are the perfect wife, you know," Stanford said. "I can't imagine why you're not already married."

"Straight men bore me," Suzannah said. "Eventually anyway. It always starts off fine, and then they become incredibly demanding. Before you know it, you're doing everything they want, and you have no life left."

"We won't be like that," Stanford said. "This is perfect."

Suzannah stood up. "I'm off to bed," she said. "I want to get up early and ski. Sure you won't join me?"

"On the slopes? Never," Stanford said. "But you must promise me one thing. That we have an evening exactly like this one tomorrow night."

"Certainly."

"You really are the most wonderful cook. Where did you learn to cook like that?"

"Paris."

Stanford stood up. "Good night, my dear."

"Good night," she said. Stanford leaned forward and gave her a chaste kiss on the cheek. "Until tomorrow," he said, giving her a little wave as she walked to her room.

A few minutes later, Stanford went to his room. But he did not go to sleep. Instead, he turned on his computer and checked his e-mail. As he had hoped, there was a message for him. He picked up the phone and called a taxi. Then he waited by the window.

When the taxi pulled up, he slipped out of the house. "Caribou Club," he said to the driver.

And then it was like a bad dream. The taxi took him to a cobblestoned street in the center of town. Stanford walked through a narrow alley lined with tiny shops, then went in a door and down some stairs. A blond woman, who was probably forty but through the miracles of facial plastic surgery and breast implants looked five years younger, was standing behind a wooden podium.

"I'm meeting someone here," Stanford said. "But I don't know what his name is."

The woman looked at him suspiciously.

"I'm Stanford Blatch. The screenplay writer?" he said.

"Yes?" she said.

Stanford smiled. "Did you ever see the movie *Fashion Victims*?"

"Oh!" the woman said. "I loved that movie. Did you write that?"

"Yes I did."

"What are you working on now?" she asked.

"I'm thinking about doing a movie about people who have too much plastic surgery," he said.

"Omigod," she said. "My best friend . . ."

"I think I see my friends now," Stanford said.

In one corner, two men and a woman were drinking and laughing. Stanford approached. The guy in the middle looked up. He was about forty, tanned, with bleached hair. Stanford could see that he'd had his nose and cheeks done, and probably had hair plugs. "Hercules?" Stanford asked.

"Yeah," the guy said.

"I'm Prometheus," Stanford said.

The girl looked from the guy back to Stanford. "Hercules? Prometheus?" she asked. She had an obnoxious, nasally voice, and she was wearing a cheap, fuzzy, pink sweater. Not good enough to clean my grandmother's attic, Stanford thought, and decided to ignore her.

"You don't look like much of a Prometheus to me," Hercules said, taking in Stanford's long hair and fancy clothes.

"Are you going to invite me to sit down and have a drink, or are you just going to insult me?" Stanford asked.

"I think we should just insult you," said the other guy. "Who are you, anyway?"

"Another loser I met on the Internet," said Hercules. He took a sip of his drink.

"Takes one to know one," Stanford said.

"Man. I don't even know how to turn on a computer," the girl said.

"I check out every guy who comes through Aspen. Then I take my pick," said Hercules. "And you don't . . . make the cut."

"Well, at least I know how to pick my plastic surgeon," Stanford said calmly. "It's such a shame when people remember your plastic surgery and not you." He smiled. "Have a pleasant evening. *Gentlemen.*"

CAN YOU KEEP A SECRET?

Carrie and Mr. Big were having lunch outside at the Little Nell when they ran into Rock Gibralter. And Tyler Kydd.

Tyler Kydd saw them first. He wasn't handsome like Mr. Big. But he was cool. Craggy face. Longish blond hair. Lanky body. He caught Carrie's eye. "Uh oh," she thought.

Then Mr. Big said, "Rocko. Baby." And stuck his cigar in his mouth and slapped Rock on the back and pumped his hand.

"I've been looking for you guys," Rock said. And then: "Do you know Tyler Kydd?"

"No, man," Mr. Big said. "But I know your movies. When are you gonna get the girl?" They all laughed and sat down.

"Big just got accosted by a mountie," Carrie said. "For smoking his cigar on the gondola."

"Oh, man," Mr. Big said. "Every day, I'm smoking my cigar on the gondola and the girl keeps telling me there's no smoking. I just say it's not lit," he said to Tyler.

"Cuban?" Tyler asked.

"Yeah, man."

"Something like that happened to me once in Gstaad," Tyler said to Carrie. She thought to herself, He would be perfect for Samantha Jones.

"Hey baby, can you pass the salt?" Mr. Big said, patting her leg.

She leaned over and they kissed briefly on the lips. "Excuse me," she said.

She got up. She went into the ladies' room. She was a little nervous. If I wasn't with Mr. Big . . . , she thought. And then she thought that it wasn't even a good idea to think that way.

When she came out, Tyler was smoking a cigar with Mr. Big.

"Hey baby, guess what?" Mr. Big said. "Tyler's invited us to go snowmobiling. Then we're going to go to his house and race go-carts."

"Go-carts?" Carrie said.

"I've got a frozen lake on my property."

"Isn't that great?" Mr. Big said.

"Yeah," Carrie said. "Great."

That night, Carrie and Mr. Big had dinner with Stanford and Suzannah. All through the dinner, whenever Suzannah said anything, Stanford would lean over and say, "Isn't she just terrific?" He held her hand, and she said, "Oh Stanford. You're such a dope," and laughed and removed her hand to lift her wineglass.

"I'm so glad you've finally come over to the other side," Mr. Big said.

"Who said anything about that?" Suzannah said.

"I'll always be a queen, if that's what you're worried about," Stanford said.

Carrie went outside to smoke a cigarette. A woman came up to her. "Can I have a light?" she said. And it turned out the woman was Brigid. The obnoxious woman from the bridal shower last summer.

"Carrie?" she said. "Is that you?"

"Brigid!" Carrie said. "What are you doing here?"

"Skiing," Brigid said. And then, glancing around as if she were afraid of being overheard, she said, "With my husband. And no kids. We left the kids at my mother's house."

"Weren't you, um, pregnant?" Carrie asked.

"Miscarriage," Brigid said. She glanced around again. "Say, you wouldn't happen to have an extra cigarette in addition to that match, would you?"

"Sure," Carrie said.

"I haven't smoked for years. Years. But I *need* this." She inhaled deeply. "When I used to smoke, I only smoked Marlboro Reds."

Carrie gave her an evil smile. "Of course you did." She dropped her cigarette on the sidewalk and mashed it with her boot.

"Can you keep a secret?" Brigid asked.

"Yeah . . . ," Carrie said.

"Well." Brigid took another deep drag and blew the smoke out her nose. "I didn't go home last night."

"Uh huh," Carrie said, thinking, Why are you telling me this?

"No. I mean, *I didn't go home.*"

"Oh," Carrie said.

"That's right. I didn't spend the night with my husband. I stayed out all night. I slept, I actually *spent the night,* in Snowmass."

"I see," Carrie said, nodding. "Were you, uh, you know. Doing drugs?"

"Nooooo," Brigid said. "I was with a guy. Not my husband."

"You mean you . . ."

"Yes. *I slept with another guy.*"

"That's amazing," Carrie said. She lit another cigarette.

"I haven't slept with another man for fifteen years. Well, okay, maybe seven," Brigid said. "But I'm thinking about leaving my husband, and I had this incredibly amazing ski instructor, and I just decided, what am I doing with my life? So I told my husband I was going out, and I went to meet him, Justin, the ski instructor, at this bar in Snowmass, and then I went back to his little apartment with him and we had sex all night."

"Does your, uh, husband know about this?" Carrie asked.

"I told him this morning when I got in. But what could he do? I'd already done it."

"Jeez," Carrie said.

"He's inside the restaurant now," Brigid said. "Freaking out. And I told Justin I would meet him later." Brigid took a final drag on the cigarette. "You know, I knew you were the one person who would understand," she said. "I want to call you. When we get back. We should go out and have a girl's night."

"Great," Carrie said. Thinking, That's just what I need.

"MY FEET ARE COLD"

They went snowmobiling with Tyler and Rock. Tyler and Mr. Big drove too fast and some people yelled at them. Then Mr. Big made Carrie ride on the back of his snowmobile and she kept screaming at him to let her off because she was afraid they were going to tip over.

A couple of days later, they went to Tyler's house. It was a fort in the woods that had once belonged to a porno star. There were bearskin rugs and animal heads mounted on the walls. They drank shots of tequila and shot bows and arrows. They raced the go-carts, and Carrie won every race. Then they went for a walk in the woods.

"I want to go in. My feet are cold," Mr. Big said.

"Why didn't you wear sensible shoes?" Carrie said. She stood at the edge of the stream, pushing snow in with the toe of her boot. "Don't," Mr. Big said. "You'll fall in."

"No I won't," Carrie said. She kicked more snow into the stream, watching it melt in the water. "I always used to do this when I was a kid."

Tyler was standing behind them. "Always pushing the limits," he said. Carrie turned, and they stared at each other for the briefest second.

On their last night, they all went to a party at the home of Bob Milo, a famous Hollywood movie star. His house was up on the other side of the mountain, and to get there, they had to park the car and ride on snowmobiles. The house and grounds were decorated with Japanese lanterns, even though it was February and snowy. Inside the house, there was a sort of grotto with koi swimming in it and a bridge you had to walk over to get to the living room.

Bob Milo was holding forth in front of the fireplace. His girlfriend and his soon-to-be-ex-wife were there, looking almost like twins except the wife was about five years older than the girlfriend. Bob Milo was dressed in a sweater and the bottom half of his long underwear. He was about five feet tall and was wearing felt slippers with pointy toes, so that he resembled an elf.

"I work out six hours a day," he was saying, when Stanford interrupted him. "Excuse me," he said, "but who decorated the interior of your jet?"

Milo glared at him.

"No, I mean it," Stanford said. "I'm thinking of buying a private jet, and I want to be sure to get the right decorator."

Carrie was sitting at a table, eating her way through a pile of stone crab claws and shrimp. She was talking to Rock, and they were both being horrible little cats, whispering jokes about the party and laughing, being more and more obnoxious. Mr. Big was sitting next to Carrie, talking to Tyler, who had two women draped over him. Carrie looked at Tyler and thought, I am so glad I don't have to deal with a man like that.

She went back to her shrimp. And then there was a sort of mini commotion and a blond girl came over, waving her arms and talking in some kind of accent, and Carrie thought, Uh oh, I've heard that voice before, and decided to ignore it.

The girl came over and practically sat in Mr. Big's lap. They were both laughing about something. Carrie didn't turn around. Then someone said to Mr. Big, "How long have you two known each other?"

"I don't know. How long?" the girl said to Mr. Big.

"Maybe two years?" Mr. Big said.

"We bonded at Le Palais. In Paris," the girl said.

Carrie turned. She smiled. "Hello Ray," she said. "What did you do? Give him one of your famous blow jobs in the corner?"

There was a moment of shocked silence, and then everyone began laughing hysterically, except Ray. "What are you talking about? What do you mean?" she went on and on in her stupid accent.

"It's a joke," Carrie said. "Don't you get it?"

"If that's your idea of humor, honey, it's *not* funny."

"Really," Carrie said. "So sorry. Everyone else seems to think it was hysterical. Now, if you don't mind removing yourself from my boyfriend's lap, I'll get back to my conversation."

"You shouldn't have said that," Mr. Big said. He got up and walked away.

"Shit," Carrie said. She went to find him, but instead she ran into another commotion. Stanford was in the middle of the room, screaming. There was a blond man standing there, and behind him was the Bone.

"You cheap little slut," Stanford was saying to the Bone. "Did anyone ever tell you what a slut you were? How could you take up with this kind of trash?"

"Hey," the Bone said. "I just met the guy. He asked me to a party. He's a friend."

"Oh please," Stanford said. "Please. Somebody bring me a drink so I can throw it in your face."

Ray walked by with Skipper Johnson in tow. "I've always wanted my own TV show," she was saying. "By the way, did I tell you that I've had a child? I can do things with my pussy that no woman has ever done to you before."

After that, Carrie made everyone go into the bathroom and smoke marijuana, then they came out and she danced wildly with Mr. Big, and people kept coming up to them saying, "You two are the best dancers."

They left the party at one, and a bunch of people went back to their house. Carrie kept drinking and smoking pot until she could hardly walk, then she went into the bathroom and threw up and lay on the floor. She threw up again and Mr. Big came in and tried to hold her head, and she said, "Don'toush'me," and he made her get into bed and she climbed out and went back into the bathroom and threw up again. Eventually she crawled into the bedroom. She lay on the floor next to the bed for a while, and when she could lift her head, she got into bed and passed out, knowing that there were little chunks of vomit in her hair and not caring.

It was a cold, clear night. Stanford Blatch wandered in and out among the private planes in the Aspen airport. He passed the Lear jets and the Gulf Streams, the Citations and the Challengers. And as he passed each one, he touched the tail numbers, looking for a number he recognized. Looking for a plane that could take him home.

SHE STARTED CRYING

"I'm not stupid, you know," Mr. Big said. They were sitting in first class. Going back.

"I know," Carrie said.

Mr. Big took a sip of his bloody mary. He took out his paperback book. "You know, I'm actually very perceptive."

"Uh huh," Carrie said. "How's the book?"

"Not much gets by me."

"Of course not," Carrie said. "That's why you make so much money."

"I'm aware of all kinds of things going on under the surface," Mr. Big said. "And I know you liked that guy."

Carrie took a sip of her drink. "Mmmmm," she said. "What guy?"

"You know exactly who I mean. Tyler."

"Tyler?" Carrie said. She took out her book. Opened it. "I thought he was nice. And, you know. Interesting. But so what."

"You liked him," Mr. Big said casually. He opened his book.

Carrie pretended to read. "I liked him as a friend."

"I was there. I saw everything. It would be better if you didn't lie," he said.

"O-kay," Carrie said. "I was attracted to him. A *little* bit," and as soon as she said it she realized it was a mistake, she hadn't been attracted to him at all.

"I'm a grownup," Mr. Big said. He put down his book and crossed his legs. He took out a magazine from the pocket in front of him. "I can take it. It doesn't hurt me. Go back. Go back to him and live with him in his fort. You can live in a fort and shoot bows and arrows all day."

"But I don't want to live in a fort," Carrie said. She started crying. She cried into her hand with her head turned toward the window. "Why are you doing this?" she asked. "You're trying to get rid of me. You're making all this stuff up in your head so you can get rid of me."

"You *said* you were attracted to him."

"*A little bit*," Carrie hissed. "And only because you made me say it. I knew this was going to happen. I knew it." She sobbed. "As soon as we saw him, I knew you were going to think that I liked him and I never would have even thought of liking him if you didn't act like you thought I did. So then I have to spend the whole time acting like I don't like him so you don't get upset and the stupid thing is that I don't even like him to begin with. At all."

"I don't believe you," Mr. Big said.

"It's the truth. Oh Jesus," Carrie said. She turned away and cried a little more, and then she leaned over and whispered loudly in his ear, "I'm totally crazy about you and you know it. I would never want to be with anyone else. And it isn't fair. It isn't fair, you acting like this." She opened up her book.

Mr. Big patted her hand. "Don't worry about it," he said.

"Now *I'm* mad," she said.

They'd been back in New York two days when Carrie got a call from Samantha Jones. "Soooooo," she said.

"So what?" Carrie asked.

"Anything big happen in Aspen?" she asked, in this creepy, cooing voice.

"Like what?" Carrie asked.

"I was convinced you were going to come back engaged."

"Nooooo," Carrie said. She leaned back in her chair and put her feet up on the desk. "Why on earth would you think that?"

25

The Last Chapter

"Hey! Come to a party." Samantha Jones; she was calling Carrie from an art gallery in SoHo. "I haven't seen you in ages."

"I don't know," Carrie said. "I told Mr. Big I might make him dinner. He's out now, at a cocktail party . . ."

"He's out and you're waiting at home for him? Oh come *on,*" Samantha said. "He's a big boy. He can get his own dinner."

"There's the plants too."

"Plants?"

"Houseplants, actually," Carrie said. "I've developed this strange obsession. Some houseplants are grown for their foliage, but I'm not interested in foliage, only flowers."

"Flowers," Sam said. "Cute." She laughed her clear, bell-ringing laugh. "Get in a cab. You'll be gone half an hour, forty-five minutes at most."

When Carrie got to the party, Sam said, "Don't you look nice. Just like a newcaster."

"Thank you," Carrie said. "It's my new look. Early Stepford wife." She was wearing a powder blue suit with a skirt that came to her knees and fifties-style satin pumps.

"Champagne?" Sam asked, as a waiter slid by with a tray.

"No thanks. I'm trying not to drink," Carrie said.

"Good. I'll take yours then." Sam picked up two glasses off the tray. She nodded across the room at a tall, tanned woman with short blond hair. "See that girl?" she asked. "She's one of those girls who has a perfect life. Married at twenty-five to Roger, the guy next to her. The screenplay writer. His last three movies have been hits. She was just a girl, like us, not a model but beautiful—she met Roger, who I think is adorable, smart, sexy, nice, and really funny, she's never had to work, they have two kids and a nanny and a great apartment in the city and the perfect house in the Hamptons, and she's never had to worry about anything."

"So?"

"So, I hate her," Sam said. "Except, of course, she's really nice."

"What's not to be nice about?"

They watched the girl. The way she moved around the room, making small bits of conversation, leaning forward to giggle in someone's ear. Her clothes were right, her makeup was right, her hair was right, and she had about her the sort of ease that comes with a sense of unchallenged entitlement. She looked up, saw Sam and waved.

"How are you?" she asked Sam enthusiastically, coming over. "I haven't seen you since . . . the last party."

"Your husband's really big time now, isn't he?" Sam said.

"Oh yes," she said. "Last night we had dinner with ——," she said, naming a well-known Hollywood director. "I know you're not supposed to be starstruck, but it was really exciting," she said, looking at Carrie.

"And what about you?" Sam asked. "How are the kids?"

"Great. And I just got money to make my first documentary."

"Really?" Sam said. She hiked her bag up onto her shoulder. "About what?"

"This year's female political candidates. I've got some Hollywood actresses who are interested in narrating. We're going to take it to one of the networks. I'm going to have to spend a lot of time in Washington, so I told Roger and the kids they were just going to have to do without me."

"How will they manage?" Sam asked.

"Well, Sam, that's what I ask myself about you," the girl said. "I mean, with this project, I couldn't do it if I wasn't married. Roger's given me so much *self-confidence*. Anytime something goes wrong, I run into his office, screaming. I couldn't handle it if I didn't have him. I'd crumple up and never take any real risks. I don't know how you girls do it, being single for years and years."

"That makes me sick," Sam said, when the girl walked away. "Why should she get money for doing a documentary? She's never done a fucking thing in her life."

"Everybody's a rock star," Carrie said.

"I think Roger's going to need some company while she's away," Sam said. "I'd definitely marry a guy like that."

"You'd only marry a guy like that," Carrie said, lighting a cigarette. "A guy who was already married."

"You're full of shit," Sam said.

"Going out afterward?" Carrie asked.

"Dinner with ——," Sam said, naming a well-known artist. "Going home?"

"I told Big I'd cook him dinner."

"That's so cute. Cooking dinner," Sam said.

"Yeah. Sure," Carrie said. She mashed out her cigarette and went through a revolving door onto the street.

A RELATIONSHIP? HOW SILLY

Sam was having a big week. "Did you ever have one of those weeks when, I don't know how to explain it, you walk into a room and every guy wants to be with you?" she asked Carrie.

Sam went to a party where she bumped into a guy she hadn't seen for about seven years. He was one of those guys who, seven years ago, every woman on the Upper East Side had been after. He was handsome, came from a wealthy,

connected family, dated models. Now, he said, he was looking for a relationship.

At the party, Sam let him back her into a corner. He'd had
a few drinks. "I always thought you were so beautiful," he
said. "But I was scared of you."

"Scared? Of me?" Sam laughed.

"You were smart. And tough. I thought you'd rip me to
shreds."

"You're saying you thought I was a bitch."

"Not a bitch. Just that I thought I wouldn't be able to
keep up."

"And now?"

"I don't know."

"I like it when men think I'm smarter than they are," Sam
said. "Because it's usually true."

They went to dinner. More drinks. "God, Sam," he said.
"I can't believe I'm with you."

"Why not?" Sam said, holding her cocktail glass high in
the air.

"I kept reading about you in the papers. I kept wanting to
get in touch with you. But I thought, She's famous now."

"I'm not famous," Sam said. "I don't even want to *be* famous," and they started making out.

Sam touched his unmentionable, and it was a big one. A
really big one. "There's just something about those really,
really big ones," she said later to Carrie. "They make you
want to have sex."

"So did you?" Carrie asked.

"No," Sam said. "He said he wanted to go home. Then he
called the next day. He wants to have a *relationship*. Can you
believe that? It's just so *silly*."

THE TALKING PARAKEET

Carrie and Mr. Big went to Carrie's parents' house for the
weekend. In her house, everybody cooked. Mr. Big was making
a beautiful effort to get along. "I'll make the gravy," he said.

"Don't screw it up," Carrie whispered as she walked by him.

"What's wrong with my gravy? I make great gravy," Mr. Big said.

"The last time you made it, you put whiskey or something in it, and it was terrible."

"That was me," her father said.

"Oh. So sorry," Carrie said meanly. "I forgot."

Mr. Big didn't say anything. The next day, they went back to the city and had dinner with some of his friends. They were all couples who'd been married for years. Somebody started talking about parrots. How they'd had a parrot that talked.

"I went into a Woolworth's once and bought a parakeet for ten bucks and taught it how to talk," Mr. Big said.

"Parakeets can't talk," Carrie said.

"It talked," Mr. Big said. "It said, 'Hello Snippy.' That was the name of my dog."

In the car on the way home, Carrie said, "It couldn't have been a parakeet. It must have been a mynah bird."

"If I say it was a parakeet, it was a parakeet."

Carrie snorted. "That's stupid. Everyone knows that parakeets can't talk."

"It talked," Mr. Big said. He lit up a cigar. They didn't say anything the rest of the way home.

DON'T GO THERE

Carrie and Mr. Big went to the Hamptons for a weekend. It wasn't quite spring yet, and it was depressing. They lit a fire. They read their books. They rented movies. Mr. Big would watch only action movies. Carrie used to watch them with him, but now she didn't want to watch them anymore. "It's a waste of time for me," she said.

"So read," Mr. Big said.

"I'm bored with reading. I'm going to take a walk."

"I'll take a walk with you," Mr. Big said. "As soon as this movie is over."

So she sat next to him and watched the movie and sulked.

They went to the Palm for dinner. She said something, and he said, "Oh, that's stupid."

"Really? How interesting. That you should call me stupid. Especially since I'm smarter than you," Carrie said.

Mr. Big laughed. "If you think that, you're really stupid."

"Don't fuck with me," Carrie said. She leaned across the table, suddenly so angry she didn't even know who she was anymore. "If you fuck with me, I will make it my personal business to destroy you. And don't think for a second that I won't take a great deal of pleasure in doing it."

"You don't get up early enough to fuck with me," Mr. Big said.

"I don't need to. Haven't you figured that out yet?" She wiped the corner of her mouth with her napkin. *Don't go there,* she thought. *Just don't go there.* Aloud she said, "I'm sorry. I'm just a little tense."

The next morning, when they were back in the city, Mr. Big said, "Well, I'll talk to you later."

"Talk?" Carrie said. "You mean we're not going to see each other this evening?"

"I don't know," Mr. Big said. "I think maybe we should take a little break, spend a couple of days apart until you get over this mood."

"But I'm over it," Carrie said.

She called him at work. He said, "I don't know about things," and she laughed and said, "Oh, come on, silly. Isn't a person allowed to be in a bad mood? It's not the end of the world. Relationships are like that sometimes. I said I was sorry."

"I don't want any hassles."

"I promise I'll be sweet. Aren't I being sweet now? See? No more bad mood."

"I guess so," he said.

WHILE BIG'S AWAY

Time passed. Mr. Big went away on business for weeks. Carrie stayed in Mr. Big's apartment. Stanford Blatch came over sometimes, and he and Carrie would act like they were two high schoolers whose parents had gone out of town: They smoked pot and drank whiskey sours and made brownies and watched stupid movies. They made a mess, and in the morning the maid would come in and clean it all up, getting down on her hands and knees to scrub the juice stains out of the white carpet.

Samantha Jones called a couple of times. She started telling Carrie about all these interesting, famous men she was meeting and all these great parties and dinners she was going to. "What are you doing?" she'd ask, and Carrie would say, "Working, just working."

"We should go out. While Big's away . . ." Sam said. But she never made concrete plans and after a couple of times, Carrie didn't feel like talking to her. Then Carrie felt bad, so she called Samantha up and went to lunch with her. At first it was a good lunch. Then Sam started talking about all these movie projects and all these big cheeses she knew whom she was going to do business with. Carrie had her own project going, and Sam said, "It's cute, you know. It's a cute idea."

Carrie said, "What's so cute about it?"

"It's cute. It's light. You know. It's not Tolstoy."

"I'm not trying to be Tolstoy," Carrie said. But of course, she was.

"So there you go," Sam said. "Hey, I've known you forever. I should be able to tell you what I really think about something without you getting upset. It doesn't have anything to do with you."

"Really?" Carrie said. "I wonder."

"Besides," Sam said. "You're probably going to marry Mr. Big and have kids. Come on. That's what everybody wants."

"Aren't I lucky?" she said, and she picked up the check.

"I WANT THE TRUTH"

Mr. Big came back from his trip, and he and Carrie went to St. Barts for a long weekend.

The first night, she had a dream that Mr. Big was having an affair with a dark-haired girl. Carrie went to a restaurant and Mr. Big was with the girl, and the girl was sitting in Carrie's chair and she and Mr. Big were kissing. "What is going on?" Carrie demanded.

"Nothing," Mr. Big said.

"I want the truth."

"I'm in love with her. We want to be together," Mr. Big said.

Carrie had that old familiar feeling of hurt and disbelief. "Okay," she said.

She went outside and into a field. Giant horses with golden bridles came out of the sky and down the mountain. When she saw the horses, she realized that Mr. Big and his feelings about her were not important.

She woke up.

"You had a bad dream?" Mr. Big said. "Come here."

He reached out for her. "Don't touch me!" she said. "I feel sick."

The dream hung around for days afterward.

"What can I do?" Mr. Big said. "I can't compete with a dream." They were sitting on the edge of the pool with their feet in the water. The light from the sun was almost white.

"Do you think we talk enough?" Carrie asked.

"No," Mr. Big said. "No, we probably don't."

They drove around and went to the beach and to lunch and talked about how beautiful it was and how relaxed they were. They exclaimed over a hen crossing the road with two newly hatched chicks, over a tiny eel caught in a tidal pool, over the dead rats that lay squished on the sides of the roads.

"Are we friends?" Carrie asked.

"There was a time when we really were friends. When I felt like you understood my soul," Mr. Big said. They were driving on the narrow, curving, cement roads.

"A person can only make so much effort until they get tired or lose interest," Carrie said.

They didn't say anything for a while, then Carrie said: "How come you never say 'I love you'?"

"Because I'm afraid," Mr. Big said. "I'm afraid that if I say 'I love you,' you're going to think that we're going to get married." Mr. Big slowed the car down. They went over a speed bump and passed a cemetery filled with brightly colored plastic flowers. A group of bare-chested young men were standing on the side of the road, smoking. "I don't know," Mr. Big said. "What's wrong with the way things are right now?"

Later, when they were packing to go home, Mr. Big said, "Have you seen my shoes? Can you be sure to pack my shampoo?"

"No, and of course, darling," Carrie said lightly. She went into the bathroom. In the mirror, she looked good. Tan and slim and blond. She began packing up her cosmetics. Toothbrush. Face cream. His shampoo was still in the shower, and she decided to ignore it. "What if I got pregnant?" she thought. She wouldn't tell him and she'd secretly have an abortion and never talk to him again. Or she would tell him and have the abortion anyway and never talk to him again. Or she would have the kid and raise it up on her own, but that could be tricky. What if she hated him so much for not wanting to be with her that she ended up hating the kid?

She went into the bedroom and put on her high heels and straw hat. It was custom made and it cost over five hundred dollars. "Oh darling . . .," she said.

"Yes?" he asked. His back was turned. He was putting things in his suitcase.

She wanted to say, "That's it, dear. It's over. We've had a great time together. But I always feel it's better to end things on a high note. You do understand . . . ?"

Mr. Big looked up. "What?" he said. "Did you want something, baby?"

"Oh, nothing," Carrie said. "I just forgot your shampoo, that's all."

"HE'S JUST A CREEP"

Carrie drank five bloody mary's on the plane, and they fought all the way home. In the airport. In the limo. Carrie didn't shut up until he said, "Do you want me to drop you off at your place? Is that what you want?" When they got to his apartment, she called her parents. "We got into a big fight," she said. "He's just a creep. Like all men."

"Are you all right?" her father asked.

"Oh, I'm great," she said.

Then Mr. Big was nice. He made her get into pyjamas and sat with her on the couch. "When I first met you, I liked you," he said. "Then I liked you a lot. Now I . . . I've grown to love you."

"Don't make me vomit," Carrie said.

"Why me, baby?" he asked. "With all the guys you've gone out with, why do you want to pick me?"

"Who said I did?"

"What is this, a pattern?" Mr. Big said. "Now that I'm more involved, you want to bail. You want to run away. Well, I can't do anything about that."

"Yes, you can," Carrie said. "That's the whole point."

"I don't get it," Mr. Big said. "How is our relationship different from all the others you've had?"

"It's not. It's just the same," Carrie said. "So far, it's just *sufficient*."

The next morning, Mr. Big was his usual cheery self and it was annoying. "Help me pick out a tie, baby," he said, the way he always did. He brought five ties over to where Carrie was still trying to sleep, turned on the light, and handed her her glasses. He held the ties up to his suit.

Carrie glanced at them briefly. "That one," she said. She threw off the glasses and lay back against the pillows and closed her eyes.

"But you hardly even looked at them," Mr. Big said.

"That's my final decision," she said. Besides, in the end, isn't one tie very much like another?"

"Oh. You're still mad," Mr. Big said. "I don't get it. You should be happy. After last night, I think things are a lot better."

HOME SWEET HOME

"The baby's starving and the nanny left and I'm broke," Amalita said on the phone. "Bring some pizza, won't you, sweetpea, just two or three slices with pepperoni, and I'll pay you back later."

Amalita was staying in a friend-of-a-friend's apartment on the Upper East Side. It was one of those side streets Carrie knew too well: dirty brick buildings with narrow entranceways littered with takeout menus from Chinese restaurants, and on the streets, grubby people walking scruffy dogs, and in the summer, obese women sitting out on the stoops. For a long time, Carrie had thought she'd never get away from it. She bought the pizza at the same place where she always used to buy pizza, near where she'd lived for four years when she was broke. It was still the same guy with the dirty fingers making the pizza and his little wife who never said anything working the cash register.

Amalita's apartment was at the top of four rickety flights of stairs, in the back. One of those places where someone had tried to make the best of the exposed cinderblock walls and failed. "Well," Amalita said. "It's temporary. The rent is cheap. Five hundred a month."

Her daughter, a beautiful little girl with dark hair and huge blue eyes, sat on the floor in front of a pile of old newspapers and magazines turning the pages.

"Well!" Amalita said. "I never heard from Righty. After he wanted me to go on tour with him and after I sent him a book he wanted me to send him. These guys don't want a girl who's a great fuck. Or even a good fuck. They want a girl who's a bad fuck."

"I know," Carrie said.

"Look! Mama!" the girl said proudly. She pointed to a photo of Amalita at Ascot in a picture hat with Lord somebody or other.

"A Japanese businessman wanted to set me up in an apartment," Amalita said. "You know, I detest that kind of thing, but the truth is, I'm temporarily broke. The only reason I was considering doing it was for the baby. I'm trying to get her into a preschool, and I need money to pay for it. So I said yes. Two weeks pass and I haven't heard from him. Not a peep. So that just goes to show."

Amalita sat on the couch in her sweatpants, tearing off pieces of pizza. Carrie sat on a narrow wooden chair. She was wearing jeans and a T-shirt with yellow stains under the armpits. Both girls had greasy hair. "When I look back in retrospect," Amalita said, "I think, I shouldn't have slept with this guy, I shouldn't have slept with that guy. Maybe I should have done things differently."

She paused. "I know you're thinking about leaving Mr. Big. Don't. Hold on to him. Of course, you're beautiful, and you should have a million guys calling you up, wanting to be with you. But you and I, we know the truth. We know something about real life, don't we?"

"Mama!" the little girl said. She held up a magazine, pointing to a photo spread of Amalita: She was wearing a white Chanel ski suit on the slopes of St. Moritz, then getting out of a limo at a Rolling Stones concert, smiling demurely in a black suit and pearls next to a senator.

"Carrington! Not now," Amalita said, with mock severity. The little girl looked at her and giggled. She threw the magazine into the air.

It was a sunny day. The sun streamed in through the dirty windows. "Come here, sweetpea," Amalita said. "Come here and have some pizza."

"Hello, I'm home," Mr. Big said.

"Hello," Carrie said. She went to the door and kissed him. "How was the cocktail party?"

"Fine, fine."

"I'm making dinner."

"Good. I'm so glad we don't have to go out."

"Me too," she said.

"Want a drink?" he asked.

"No thanks," she said. "Just maybe a glass of wine with dinner."

She lit candles, and they sat in the dining room. Carrie sat up very straight in her chair. Mr. Big talked on and on about some deal he was in the middle of doing, and Carrie stared at him and nodded and made encouraging noises. But she wasn't really paying attention.

When he was finished talking, she said: "I'm so excited. The amaryllis finally bloomed. It has four flowers."

"Four flowers," Mr. Big said. And then: "I'm so happy you've taken an interest in plants."

"Yes. Isn't it nice?" Carrie said. "It's amazing the way they grow if you just pay a bit of attention."

Epilogue

Stanford Blatch's movie *Fashion Victims* eventually raked in over $200 million worldwide. Stanford recently bought a Challenger and had the interior decorated like Elizabeth Taylor's boudoir in *Cleopatra*.

River Wilde is still working on his novel. In it, Mr. Big roasts a child and eats it. Stanford Blatch shows up everywhere, but nothing ever happens to him.

Samantha Jones decided to give up on New York. She went out to L.A. for the Oscars and met Tyler Kydd at a party where they were both naked in the swimming pool. They're now living together, but he has vowed that he'll never marry her because after he failed to win the Academy Award for best actor, Samantha said, "Well, that's because the movie was just cute." Nevertheless, Sam is producing his next movie—an art flick.

Amalita Amalfi's daughter got into the prestigious Kitford preschool in New York. Amalita started her own consulting firm. She has three employees, as well as a small staff—a driver, a nanny, and a maid. She recently bought her daughter her first designer suit.

The Bone is still a male model.

Magda, the novelist, went to a party to celebrate the publication of a calendar featuring New York City firefighters. Mr. September, thirty-three, picked her up, and they've been inseparable ever since.

Packard and Amanda Deale had another child, a girl. They're raising their children to be geniuses. The last time Carrie had dinner at their house, Packard said to Chester, "Do you realize that honey-roasted peanuts are a phenomenon of our lifetime?" Chester nodded.

Brigid Chalmers left her husband. She was last seen at the Tunnel at four A.M., dancing wildly with Barkley.

All of the perennial bachelors are still available.

Belle and Newbert went to a coed baby shower on Fifth Avenue. Newbert insisted on wearing a funny, striped Cat-in-the-Hat chapeau, then he made everyone drink shots of tequila while he danced on a credenza. The stereo blew out just as Newbert fell out the fifth-story window—luckily, he landed on the awning. During the two months Newbert was in traction, Belle became a president at her bank. She is still not pregnant.

After spending the night with Ray, Skipper Johnson came back to New York and disappeared. He resurfaced after two months, telling everyone that he was "totally in love."

Mr. Marvelous was named as the father of a child out of wedlock. He made the mother take a DNA test, and it turned out the kid wasn't his.

Carrie and Mr. Big are still together.